Simula SpringerBriefs on Computing

Volume 5

More information about this series at http://www.springer.com/series/13548

Torleif Halkjelsvik · Magne Jørgensen

Time Predictions

Understanding and Avoiding Unrealism
in Project Planning and Everyday Life

Torleif Halkjelsvik
Norwegian Institute of Public Health
Oslo
Norway

Magne Jørgensen
Department of Software Engineering
Simula Research Laboratory
Fornebu
Norway

Simula SpringerBriefs on Computing
ISBN 978-3-319-74952-5   ISBN 978-3-319-74953-2   (eBook)
https://doi.org/10.1007/978-3-319-74953-2

Library of Congress Control Number: 2018932516

Printed on acid-free paper

This Springer imprint is published by the registered company Springer International Publishing AG part of Springer Nature
The registered company address is: Gewerbestrasse 11, 6330 Cham, Switzerland

Foreword

Dear reader,

Our aim with the series *Simula SpringerBriefs on Computing* is to provide compact introductions to selected fields of computing. Although the topic of the present volume is important within computing, the authors take a broader approach and draw on research from psychology, forecasting, management science, and software engineering when summarizing knowledge about how to make realistic time predictions. The book is suitable for students, researchers, professionals, and others interested in a concise introduction to the science of time predictions. Entering a new field of research can be quite demanding for graduate students, postdocs, and experienced researchers alike: the process often involves reading hundreds of papers, and the methods, results, and notation styles used often vary considerably, which makes for a time-consuming and potentially frustrating experience. The briefs in this series are meant to ease the process by introducing and explaining important concepts and theories in a relatively narrow field, and by posing critical questions on the fundamentals of that field. A typical brief in this series should be around 100 pages and should be well suited as material for a research seminar in a well-defined and limited area of computing.

We have decided to publish all items in this series under the SpringerOpen framework, as this will allow authors to use the series to publish an initial version of their manuscript that could subsequently evolve into a full-scale book on a broader theme. Since the briefs are freely available online, the authors will not receive any direct income from the sales; however, remuneration is provided for every completed manuscript. Briefs are written on the basis of an invitation from a member of the editorial board. Suggestions for possible topics are most welcome and can be sent to aslak@simula.no.

January 2016

Prof. Aslak Tveito
CEO
Simula Research Laboratory

Dr. Martin Peters
Executive Editor Mathematics
Springer Heidelberg, Germany

Preface

A project planned to take six months may need more than one year, and a task believed to be finished in 5 minutes sometimes takes more than 20. Research has identified a large set of factors and situations that affect our time predictions, often in ways that make them overoptimistic. Reading this book will make you aware of these factors and guide you in using methods leading to more realistic time predictions. The book will also reveal how easy it is to trick yourself, your colleagues, and your friends into giving overoptimistic time predictions, and the negative consequences of doing so.

Large parts of the book are directed towards people who are interested in achieving more realistic time predictions in their professional life. They could be project managers, graphic designers, architects, engineers, film producers, consultants, software developers, or any other professional in need of realistic time usage predictions. You will, however, also benefit from reading this book if you have a general interest in judgement and decision-making or want to improve your ability to predict and plan ahead in your daily life.

The main emphasis of the book is not on formal (mathematical) models for time predictions but on *judgement-based time predictions*. In the literature on the professional prediction of time usage, this type of prediction is often called *expert estimation*. Judgement-based time predictions may involve analytical reasoning, searches for similar cases, the use of historical data, the use of expert knowledge about the task, and, in some cases, pure intuition or gut feeling. Judgement-based time predictions are, in both daily and professional life, much more common than model-based ones. In spite of that, the literature on time predictions has mainly been about the formal models. Hardly any previous book has focused on judgement-based time predictions.

When we selected the topics to be included, we emphasized topics we thought would be interesting and entertaining and could at the same time guide the reader towards improved time predictions. Although the selection of topics is based on a systematic review of relevant research,[1] it is likely to have been biased towards our own research on time predictions. That is the privilege of authoring a book. On some of the topics we address, only a few research studies have been published, sometimes only one. The results and recommendations based on such limited evidence should be taken with a grain of salt, so please use your common sense if advice or a result sounds unreasonable in your context.

The terminology used when talking about time predictions is far from standardized. Other terms are *effort estimation, time forecasts,* and *performance time predictions.* We will use the term *time usage prediction* or just *time prediction* in this book. Although the book's focus is on how much work a task or project requires, we also add results on the prediction of the point in time (completion time) and the number of days (duration) in which we predict the work to be completed.

The book starts with a brief chapter on prediction successes and disasters, illustrating how poorly and how well people can be at predicting time (Chap. 1). We then reflect on how judgement-based time predictions are made and how central they are to our lives (Chap. 2). If you are mainly interested in the practical aspects of time predictions, you may want to skip these chapters and go directly to Chap. 3. That chapter describes the basis for time predictions, with an emphasis on the importance of probability-based thinking. A good grasp of this chapter is important for an understanding of what comes later. The chapter on overoptimism (Chap. 4) gives several possible explanations of why time predictions are often overoptimistic. As you will learn here, a tendency towards overoptimistic time predictions is not necessarily caused by a disposition towards overoptimism and may have many other explanations. Chapter 5 reviews common time prediction biases, their importance, and when they are likely to occur. An awareness of these biases is important to improve time prediction processes.

In many situations, a simple number stating how many work hours are required is not enough. One would also like to know something about the confidence in and the uncertainty of the time prediction. We have, therefore, included a chapter reporting what is known about our tendency to be overconfident (Chap. 6), that is, the tendency to think that our time predictions are more accurate than they are. In Chap. 7, we describe how to improve the accuracy of time usage predictions through the use of evidence-based techniques, methods, and principles. The two latter chapters are the most practically oriented. If you just want advice on how to improve time prediction and uncertainty assessments, these are the main parts to read. Finally, we include a guide to selecting time prediction methods (Chap. 8) and a chapter describing how easy it is to influence people into making overoptimistic time predictions (Chap. 9).

Besides the authors (the sequence of authorship was determined based on coin flips), a number of people have contributed to this book. In particular, we would like to thank Karl Halvor Teigen, Scott Armstrong, and Jostein Rise for valuable

---

[1] Halkjelsvik, T., & Jørgensen, M. (2012). From origami to software development: A review of studies on judgment-based predictions of performance time. *Psychological Bulletin, 138*(2), 238.

input. We are also grateful for valuable discussions and input from previous and current research colleagues at Simula Research Laboratory and elsewhere: Stein Grimstad, Dag Sjøberg, Kjetil Moløkken-Østvold, Martin Shepperd, Emila Mendes, Barbara Kitchenham, Geir Kirkebøen, Tanja Gruschke, Bjørn Faugli, Barry Bohem, Erik Løhre, and Alf Børre Kanten. When this book refers to 'our research', this is very often work done in collaboration with the above colleagues. Last but not least, we thank Nina Olsen, Kjell Nybråten, and other colleagues at Scienta for lunch and lunch discussions while writing the book.

We hope that you will enjoy the book and that your time predictions will improve. If not, you may at least gain better insight into why your time predictions are not as good as you would hope for. Have a good read!

Oslo, Norway   Torleif Halkjelsvik
Fornebu, Norway   Magne Jørgensen

Contents

Chapter 1
Introduction

1.1 A Prediction Success

The time prediction and planning capacity of the human race is particularly evident in some of the early great constructions. An excellent example is the building of the Great Pyramid of Giza, around 4500 years ago. We do not know much about the methods they used to predict the time needed and how they managed to finish the pyramid before the pharaoh's death. Most likely, their time and resource predictions were influenced by experience from building previous pyramids. However, even if they could use previous experience, they would have to adjust the predictions for differences in the pyramid's size and location and the availability of resources. This is not an easy task, even for today's construction planners, with better tools and more historical data.

The achievements of the pyramid planners are even more impressive given that the coordination of building activities required accurate time predictions of work done by thousands of people. The building productivity of the Great Pyramid of Giza has been estimated at about one block per minute during the 10 years of the pyramid's actual construction [1]. The blocks had an average weight of 2.5 tons and had to be put in place with millimetre precision. There may have been as many as 15,000 pyramid workers and 45,000 people to support their work with catering, administration, and transport, which means that up to 4% of the population of Egypt was occupied with pyramid building. Without accurate time predictions of the activities involved, it would have been impossible to coordinate and ensure the efficient use of resources.

The project manager in charge was Hemineu, a relative of the pharaoh. Hemineu must have been a truly skilled project leader and also good at selecting people around him able to provide accurate predictions of time usage and create realistic plans for the work. Much of what is considered today to be good project time prediction and planning practices was already in place at that time: the decomposition of large projects into smaller tasks that can be better analysed and managed, inspections and the quality assurance of plans and time predictions, early feedback to improve the accuracy of time predictions, and, when needed, replanning [2].

© The Author(s) 2018
T. Halkjelsvik and M. Jørgensen, *Time Predictions*, Simula SpringerBriefs on Computing 5, https://doi.org/10.1007/978-3-319-74953-2_1

1.2   Prediction Disasters

While there are great successes in the history of time predictions, there is no shortage of time prediction disasters. In contrast to the successful construction of the Great Pyramid of Giza, several Egyptian pyramids did not finish in time, cost much more than predicted, and were left unfinished.

The early occurrence of overoptimistic time predictions is nicely illustrated by the following contract on a house repair dating back to 487 BC in Mesopotamia: 'In case the house is unfinished by Iskhuya after the first day of Tebet, Shamash-iddin shall receive four shekels of money in cash into his possession at the hands of Iskhuya' [3]. Clearly, people in Mesopotamia, one of the first civilizations, were familiar with contractors not delivering at the promised time.

Much later, large, innovative construction projects such as the medieval Basilica di San Lorenzo in Florence, the Sagrada Familia cathedral in Barcelona, and the Suez Canal experienced huge time and cost overruns. The cost predictions of the Olympic Games, have had an average cost overrun of 252% for the Summer Olympics and 135% for the Winter Olympics, and no cost prediction for any Olympic Games so far has ever been on the pessimistic side [4]. The then mayor of Montreal, Jean Drapeau, is infamous for predicting that the Winter Olympics in Montreal in 1976 could 'no more lose money than a man can have a baby' [5]. The Olympics in Montreal resulted in a debt of over $1 billion, which took the Montreal citizens more than 30 years to pay back.

Sometimes, unrealistic time predictions lead to deadly disasters. When Napoleon invaded Russia in 1812, he predicted that the war would be won in 20–30 days. Consequently, he brought food for his soldiers and horses for only about 30 days. When returning not 30 days but five months later, hundreds of thousands of his soldiers and most of his horses had died as a direct or indirect consequence of a shortage of food. This unrealistic time prediction resulting in a lack of food may have been a major reason for Napoleon losing the war. It led to lack of discipline and riots by hungry soldiers and slowed the troops' movements [6]. More than 100 years later, Hitler made a similar overoptimistic time prediction when invading Russia, with a similar outcome. More recently, other superpowers have made overoptimistic time predictions about how soon they would be able to complete their military invasions and start the withdrawal. Learning from history is hard. Huge, disastrous time prediction mistakes do not seem to prevent new failures.

The large number of time prediction failures throughout history may give the impression that our time prediction ability is very poor and that failures are much more common than the few successes that come to mind. This is, we think, an unfair evaluation. The human ability to predict time usage is generally highly impressive. It has enabled us to succeed with a variety of important goals, from controlling complex construction work to coordinating family parties. There is no doubt that the human capacity for time prediction is amazingly good and extremely useful. Unfortunately, it sometimes fails us.

References

1. Illig H, Löhner F (1993) Der Bau der Cheops-Pyramide: Nach der Rampenzeit. Mantis Verlag, Berlin
2. Kozak-Holland M (2011) The history of project management. Multi-Media Publications, Toronto
3. Fordham University Mesopotamia Contracts. legacy.fordham.edu/halsall/ancient/mesopotamia-contracts.asp. Accessed March 2017
4. Flyvbjerg B, Stewart A (2012) Olympic proportions: cost and cost overrun at the Olympics 1960–2012. Saïd Business School working papers, University of Oxford. https://papers.ssrn.com/sol3/papers.cfm?abstract_id=2238053. Accessed March 2017
5. Wikipedia: The free encyclopedia Jean Drapeau. https://en.wikipedia.org/wiki/Jean_Drapeau. Accessed Nov 2017
6. Nafziger G (1988) Napoleon's invasion of Russia. Presidio Press, Novato, CA

Chapter 2
How We Predict Time Usage

2.1 Mental Time Travel

We associate the human memory with the past, because memories are established in the past. While it is true that our memories are about things in the past, their purpose is to help us predict and manage the future. The recollection of a positive experience makes us approach similar events and an unfortunate encounter with a hot cooking plate helps us avoid harm in the future. Thus, we learn from experience and update our memory, consciously and unconsciously, for the sake of the future. The future is, however, seldom or never identical to the past and our brain has developed extreme flexibility in the way it handles memories. We can, for example, use our memories to simulate future outcomes before they have happened. This requires a high degree of flexibility and malleability of memories. We are able to combine, adjust, and manipulate memories to foresee the future. Memory is so flexible that one can make people vividly recall childhood hot air balloon flights that never happened and make them believe the event actually took place [1]. An even more surprising finding is that, through the use of interrogation techniques, innocent people can be convinced that they have carried out a crime they never did [2]. On the positive side, the flexibility of memories gives us the capacity to manipulate elements of the past in a way that enables us to travel into possible futures. This is very much what time prediction is all about: manipulating memories, perhaps together with more objective historical data, to simulate possible future outcomes. While physical time travel is still not possible, mental time travel is not only possible but also something at which we excel.

The ability to use our memory for planning and predictions, including mental time travel (*chronesthesia*), seems to make its first appearance between the age of three and four years [3]. Before that, children typically do not understand or respond meaningfully to questions about the future or to questions about the sequence of previously experienced events. The capacity of mental time travel is not a unique human ability. Great apes, such as the chimpanzees, and a few other animals seem to have this ability as well [4]. It seems, however, to be much more advanced among

© The Author(s) 2018
T. Halkjelsvik and M. Jørgensen, *Time Predictions*, Simula SpringerBriefs
on Computing 5, https://doi.org/10.1007/978-3-319-74953-2_2

humans [5] and we may turn out to be the only species with the ability to believe in and prepare for more than one potential future.[1]

The importance of mental time travel becomes even clearer when observing those who have lost this ability. This is the case for people with certain memory disorders, such as Korsakoff's syndrome [7]. Without the mental time travel ability, they are unable to create plans and take care of themselves, and also experience loss of self-identity and develop depression. The ability to conduct mental time travel is consequently not only a precondition for good predictions but also essential in defining and experiencing who we are as human beings.

Take home message 1: The main purpose of remembering the past is to enable predictions about the future, including time predictions.

Take home message 2: An advanced ability to forethink an event or mentally travel into the future is one of the defining features of human beings.

2.2   How Did You Make that Prediction?

Predictions are manipulations of memories. They connect our previous experiences with ideas about the future [8]. What do we know about which memories we use and how we connect the past and future when predicting time? What has happened when a person thinks that 30 work hours is a reasonable time usage prediction? How did this person's memories turn into a number of work hours? The simple and honest answer is that we do not know much about these issues.

The main reason for not knowing much about what is going on is that our time prediction processes are largely unconscious. Just as most people do not really know *how* they ride a bicycle (they incorrectly think it is easy to master modified bicycles, where the wheel turns right when the handlebars are turned left and vice versa [9]), people predict time without being able to correctly explain how they do so.[2] The unconscious nature of judgement-based predictions also means that we are largely unable to control how we derive our time predictions. This is clearly demonstrated in studies where people are exposed to misleading or irrelevant information and this occurrence affects their time predictions [10]. Typically, people will not even realize or admit that their time predictions have been affected by the misleading or irrelevant information. Even worse, a warning that misleading information will be present along with instructions not to take the information into account does not help much either [11]. People are often surprised when learning that misleading and irrelevant information has affected their judgement, which suggests that people

---

[1] In a study with adult apes and human children as participants, a grape could fall from two different locations. The apes and two-year-olds prepared to catch the grape from one of the locations, whereas the three- and four-year-old children prepared for both possibilities. See [6].

[2] This does not rule out that many people *think* they know how they predict time. We are very good at rationalizing, that is, inventing a plausible reason for what we think after we know what we think.

believe they are in control of their judgement-based time predictions when, in reality, they are not.

An important step towards better time predictions is, therefore, to accept that we lack full control of how we think about, recall, and judge future time usage. Accepting this fact makes us, amongst other things, more likely to avoid situations and information that distort our time predictions.

Even if people do not know where their time predictions come from, they sometimes seem to be aware of situations that make overoptimistic judgements likely. When interviewing software professionals, we found that some of them described a gut feeling about how much time is needed as the *starting point* for their time predictions. They used their gut feeling but adjusted it to reflect their previous experience about the typical overoptimism or overpessimism of previous time predictions in similar situations. As one of them stated, 'I feel this will take 40 hours. I have, however, experienced that my initial judgement is typically about 50% too low in situations like this. The time prediction I think is realistic is consequently 60 hours'. An acquaintance who works as a carpenter also said, 'I judge how much time I am sure not to exceed. Then I double this'. These statements gives no information about how the initial prediction is obtained, but they suggest that, even if we are not able to know how the initial, judgement-based time prediction was derived, we may be able to improve it through consciously controlled adjustments based on previous experiences in similar contexts. The accuracy of a time prediction strategy of this type, using the initial time prediction as a starting point and adjusting it for typical bias in similar situations, has not yet been evaluated in research.

Take home message 1: We do not know much about the mental processes leading to judgement-based time predictions. The unconscious mental processes involved are difficult to identify and describe.

Take home message 2: People tend to believe that they are more in control of their time prediction processes and less affected by misleading and irrelevant information than they really are.

Take home message 3: Knowing about one's own time prediction biases, for example, knowledge about situations leading to overoptimism, makes it possible to adjust for them and improve the realism of time predictions.

2.3 Time Predictions Are Everywhere

Many time predictions are trivial and go unnoticed, such as deciding when to leave home to be on time for a meeting, deciding whether one has time to write another email before leaving work, and predicting how much the traffic jam will slow you down. Other time predictions are more critical, such as whether one is able to finish important work on a product before the promised delivery date. We do not know much about the total number of time predictions people typically make every day, but it is likely to be high, perhaps much higher than most would think. In addition, our brain makes many time usage-related calculations that we may not classify as time predictions. When, for example, you manage to avoid hitting a car moving towards you when overtaking a slower car, this is partly due to successful predictions of the time it takes to return to your lane.[3]

We once asked students to write down two examples of situations involving predictions of time. Most frequently, the students gave time prediction examples related to transportation from one place to another and preparing oneself for activities. Interestingly, the students included time predictions not only of the type *how long will it take to...* but also of the type *how much can I do before....* This second type is not always thought about as a time prediction but it requires very much the same use of memory to assess the correspondence between an amount of work and an amount of time. As we will see later in this book, the second type of time prediction has both advantages and challenges.

Take home message: We make numerous time predictions each day. Many of them, probably most, go unnoticed.

2.4   How Good Are We at Predicting Time?

Are people typically overoptimistic when predicting time? How accurate are we in predicting time? These questions are harder to answer than it first appears. In our review on time prediction studies [13], we systematically searched for studies reporting accuracy and bias. Many studies noted only the level of bias, that is, the average tendency of predicting a too low or a too high time usage. Fewer studies included the level of accuracy, which is the average time prediction error irrespective of whether the prediction is too high or too low.[4] Unbiased time predictions do not mean that the predictions are accurate: One half could be far above the actual times and the other half far below but these inaccurate predictions would result in a zero bias if they balance each other out.

When looking at studies that do report the level of accuracy, we typically find an average time prediction error of 20–30% and great variation in time prediction accuracy, depending on the situation.

How *good* an average time prediction error of 20–30% is depends on the context. How accurate time predictions do we need? How complex is the task we are predicting? How much is possible to know about the task's completion? How much

---

[3]To be fair, such instances of timing are not necessarily time predictions. For example, it has been shown that baseball players running to catch the ball do not make sophisticated calculations of the path of the ball and the point in time when the ball with reach a certain spot. Instead, they continuously adjust their speed according to the angle of the ball. See [12].

[4]The level of accuracy is based on the unsigned error. If, for example, we have one project with a time prediction that is 10% too high and another with a time prediction that is 10% too low, the average time prediction error is 10%, while the average bias is 0%.

can we affect the actual time usage to fit the prediction? Predicting the required time usage to complete a complex and innovative construction project with many dependencies between tasks, little flexibility in deliveries, and a great deal of uncertainty with an average 20–30% error margin does not seem bad at all. Repeatedly spending 30% more time than predicted when walking the same path to the bus from home, which should be easy to predict, may, on the other hand, suggest poor time prediction skills. Our general observation based on the review of available studies is that, despite numerous horror stories about large cost and time overruns, most professional domains seemed to be, on average, quite accurate when predicting cost and time usage. It is mainly when asked for time predictions in contexts in which we have little prior experience that time predictions errors are high.

How *biased* are people's time predictions? Do people, as many would expect, typically give overoptimistic time usage predictions? As with results for accuracy, our literature review documented large variations in time prediction bias, depending on the situation. For example, when overoptimistic time predictions result in strong negative consequences, such as angry customers waiting for food, people tend to give overpessimistic time predictions. Across all reported tasks and projects, we did not find a general tendency towards either overoptimistic or overpessimistic time predictions. Reports from studies of everyday tasks, conducted in laboratory settings, instead suggested that the time predictions, on average, were unbiased. Even time predictions collected in several professional contexts, such as time predictions for smaller software development tasks, did not show a tendency towards too low time predictions. Does this mean that the common impression that people tend to make overoptimistic time predictions is wrong?

To understand and explain the contrast between the research evidence and the common belief in overoptimistic time predictions, it is useful to take a closer look at the context of the predictions. Tasks conducted as part of empirical experiments in a laboratory setting are frequently predicted with no bias. To be completed in a laboratory setting, however, the tasks are usually relatively short and involve few or no unexpected obstacles. Everyday tasks outside the laboratory setting, on the other hand, are more likely to include challenges unknown before initiation of the task. When assembling a piece of furniture, one could experience the screws not fitting or a friend who came to assist being more of a nuisance than help. Given that unexpected problems are a major contributing factor to overoptimistic time predictions, the laboratory experiment data can hardly be used as evidence of a lack of overoptimistic time predictions in realistic everyday or professional settings.

In addition to the point about the lack of realism in laboratory tasks, there are at least two other reasons for a discrepancy between the belief that people are typically overoptimistic and the research finding of unbiased time predictions. First, the likelihood that people decide to initiate projects and tasks in real life increases with an optimistic view and decreases with a pessimistic view on the required time usage [14]. For example, if your partner suggests a new colour for your kitchen cabinets and you hold realistic or even pessimistic views about the amount of work involved (removing the doors, sanding, priming, three layers of paint, etc.), you may argue that the current finish is fine and the project will never be initiated. If your time prediction of the same work is highly overoptimistic and you assume the work will be easy and take hardly any time, it is much more likely that the project will be initiated. We can only evaluate the degree of time prediction optimism on completed tasks, which means that we are more likely to become aware of our optimistic rather than our realistic or pessimistic time predictions. In contrast, all participants in psychology experiments complete their assigned tasks, regardless of whether they predict the task to be complex or easy.

A second reason for a discrepancy between research results and the perception that people typically give overoptimistic time predictions is related to the fact that the actual use of time can never be less than zero, while there is, at least in theory, no upper limit to time usage. This results in a so-called right-skewed time prediction error distribution. A task predicted to require two hours can turn out to require six additional hours but not six hours less than predicted. Throughout your life, the total time overrun is consequently likely to exceed your total time underrun. Cases of extreme overruns will also stick in your mind, whereas underruns are typically less impressive and more likely to be quickly forgotten.

Returning to the results of our systematic review of time prediction bias, we did not even find a general tendency towards overoptimistic predictions in the area of software development, a domain notoriously known for cost overruns and delays. Again, however, a closer look at the data gives a more nuanced picture. We found that the median time prediction bias was dominated by a large number of small tasks, with unbiased or even overpessimistic time predictions. When including only projects of at least 100 work hours, we found the expected overoptimism with a median time overrun of about 20%. Larger projects have a higher risk of severe problems and there are more things that can be forgotten when predicting time for such projects, so it is not surprising that the time predictions of larger projects tend to be too low. The pattern also corresponds to experimental results suggesting that people are likely to overestimate the time usage of smaller tasks and underestimate that of larger tasks.

Take home message 1: The average error of time predictions, based on evidence from multiple domains, seems to be around 20–30%.

Take home message 2: Research on time prediction finds just as much overestimation as underestimation of time usage, suggesting unbiased time predictions. For larger projects, however, the time predictions tend to be biased towards being too low, with a median time overrun of about 20%.

References

1. Wade KA, Garry M, Read JD, Lindsay DS (2002) A picture is worth a thousand lies: using false photographs to create false childhood memories. Psychon Bull Rev 9(3):597–603
2. Kassin SM, Kiechel KL (1996) The social psychology of false confessions: compliance, internalization, and confabulation. Psychol Sci 7(3):125–128
3. Busby J, Suddendorf T (2005) Recalling yesterday and predicting tomorrow. Cogn Dev 20(3):362–372

4. Osvath M, Martin-Ordas G (2014) The future of future-oriented cognition in non-humans: theory and the empirical case of the great apes. Philos Trans R Soc B 369(1655). https://doi.org/10.1098/rstb.2013.0486
5. Suddendorf T, Corballis MC (2007) The evolution of foresight: what is mental time travel, and is it unique to humans? Behav Brain Sci 30(3):299–313
6. Redshaw J, Suddendorf T (2016) Children's and apes' preparatory responses to two mutually exclusive possibilities. Curr Biol 26(13):1758–1762
7. Buckner RL, Carroll DC (2007) Self-projection and the brain. Trends Cogn Sci 11(2):49–57
8. Zeithamova D, Schlichting ML, Preston AR (2012) The hippocampus and inferential reasoning: building memories to navigate future decisions. Front Hum Neurosci 6, article 70
9. SmarterEveryDay (2015) The backwards brain bicycle. youtu.be/MFzDaBzBlL0. Accessed March 2017
10. Jørgensen M, Sjøberg DI (2004) The impact of customer expectation on software development effort estimates. Int J Project Manage 22(4):317–325
11. Wilson TD, Houston CE, Etling KM, Brekke N (1996) A new look at anchoring effects: basic anchoring and its antecedents. J Exp Psychol Gen 125(4):387–402
12. McBeath MK, Shaffer DM, Kaiser MK (1995) How baseball outfielders determine where to run to catch fly balls. Science 268(5210):569
13. Halkjelsvik T, Jørgensen M (2012) From origami to software development: a review of studies on judgment-based predictions of performance time. Psychol Bull 138(2):238–271
14. Jørgensen M (2013) The influence of selection bias on effort overruns in software development projects. Inf Softw Technol 55(9):1640–1650

Chapter 3
Predictions and the Uncertainty of the Future

3.1 Precisely Wrong or Roughly Right?

A project manager states that a project will require 432 hours. Your friend sends you a text message saying that he will be at your place in 12 minutes. The precision of these time predictions is most likely misleading when interpreted according to the rules of significant digits, where the number of trailing non-zero values indicates the intended accuracy. For example, 432 hours and 12 minutes should indicate that the time prediction error is ± 1 hour and ± 1 minute—not very likely for most types of project or arrival time predictions.

Although time predictions given with high precision are wrong most of the time, they are often the type of time predictions we like to give and receive. We may react negatively if the car service responds with 'repairing your car will take between one and 10 hours' or 'it is 70% likely that the repair will take less than six hours'. Even if we know that the prediction *one to 10 hours* reflects the actual uncertainty of the work, we may easily think that the car service is incompetent or that they are not interested in doing the work. Why is this so? One reason is that we use precision as an indicator of competence and that we perceive time predictions with many trailing zeros or wide intervals as less informative and those who present them as less competent [1]. With this in mind, it is not surprising, although unfortunate, that many prefer to be precisely wrong rather than roughly right in their time predictions.

A similar observation is the basis of the *preciseness paradox* [2]. This paradox refers to the observation that we sometimes have more confidence in precise time predictions, such as *it will take four hours*, than in time predictions that takes uncertainty into account, such as *it will take between two and 20 hours*. The latter statement is more likely to be correct than the first. Still, the first may seem more believable.

Higher precision is not always rewarded, as illustrated in a recent experiment with software professionals [3]. The software professionals evaluated the relative trustworthiness of four different hypothetical time predictions, along with evaluations of the relative competence of the persons who made them. The time predictions and

© The Author(s) 2018
T. Halkjelsvik and M. Jørgensen, *Time Predictions*, Simula SpringerBriefs on Computing 5, https://doi.org/10.1007/978-3-319-74953-2_3

Table 3.1 Percentage of participants ranking software developers as the most competent, least competent, most trustworthy, and least trustworthy

Time prediction	Most competent (%)	Least competent (%)	Most trustworthy (%)	Least trustworthy (%)
Developer A: 'The work takes 1020 work hours'	6	31	7	49
Developer B: 'The work takes 1000 work hours'	11	13	7	14
Developer C: 'The work takes between 900 and 1100 work hours'	74	1	70	1
Developer D: 'The work takes between 500 and 1500 work hours'	9	55	16	36

the evaluations are presented in Table 3.1, where the percentages are the proportions of the software professionals' responses per response category.

Developer A's time prediction (1020 work hours) is the least likely to be correct. Developer D's time prediction (between 500 and 1500 work hours) is the most likely to be correct. It is reasonable to assume that developer B's time prediction has been rounded to become 1000 work hours and that developer B, for example, believes the time usage to be between 900 and 1100 work hours, that is, about the same accuracy as the interval predicted by developer C.

In this situation, the very precise time prediction of developer A was not rewarded. The software professionals did not believe that a time prediction of 1020 work hours was believable and 49% of them ranked this as the least trustworthy time prediction. Developer A's competence was evaluated to be the lowest by 31%. The respondents were, on the other hand, not impressed by the wide time prediction interval (500–1500 work hours) of developer D either. Developer D's time prediction was ranked as the least trustworthy by 36% of the respondents and that developer's competence was ranked lowest by 55%. To be *roughly right* with a wide interval consequently seems to be a poor strategy if the goal is to make people believe in your time predictions and your competence. Instead, it would be better to act as developer C and give a narrow time prediction interval. Developer C was ranked as having the most trustworthy time prediction by 74% of the respondents and as being the most competent developer by 70%. Seemingly, the question of whether one should be precisely wrong or roughly right, in terms of being interpreted as competent, is more complex than we initially thought. One can be too precise as well as too imprecise. Interestingly, developer B (1000 work hours), who may have held similar accuracy beliefs as developer C (who indicated an interval of 900–1100 work hours) was not ranked favourably.

Strictly speaking, none of the time predictions in Table 3.1 are particularly infor-mative regarding the uncertainty of the work. The point-based time predictions (1020 and 1000 work hours) have no explicit information about uncertainty and the interval-based time predictions (900–1100 and 500–1500 work hours) do not specify the probability of the actual time usage being within these intervals. Is it 99% likely, 90%, 80%, or only 50% likely that the intervals will include the actual time usage? In the next sections, we will discuss how to make, interpret, and communicate time predictions, including their uncertainty, in more meaningful ways.

Take home message 1: When evaluating time predictions and the people producing them, greater precision is often used as an indication of greater trustworthiness and higher competence, especially in the form of narrow time prediction intervals. This happens even though such time predictions are less likely to be correct.

Take home message 2: Although people prefer precise predictions, overly precise predictions can be negatively evaluated, leading to assessments of low trustworthiness and competence, at least when assessed by people with competence in the domain.

3.2 Communication of Time Predictions

Assume that the car service tells you that the repair will be finished in four and a half hours. What does this information mean? Is the prediction meant to be a best-case prediction, assuming that the work is done by the most skilled service professional and with no unexpected problems? Is it a promise based on a worst-case time prediction? And if it is a worst-case prediction, how sure can you be that the car is actually finished in four and a half hours?

If you really need your car back in four and a half hours, the meaning of the time prediction will matter a lot. Whether the prediction was based on a best-case scenario or on experience documenting that 99% of car repairs in similar situations required less than four and a half hours will make an important difference. If the estimate was a best-case prediction, you should have a backup plan, while a 99% likelihood prediction based on past repairs should make you sufficiently safe that the car will be at your disposal when you need it.

Most people do not, as far as we have observed in various domains, explain what they mean by their time predictions. We cannot even assume that people in the same context and with similar backgrounds mean the same thing with their time predictions. We once asked software developers to give their time predictions for completion a programming task [4]. Immediately afterward, we asked them how we should interpret their time predictions. When summarizing their responses, we used the category *ideal effort* if a time prediction was based on the assumption of no unexpected problems, *most likely effort* if a time prediction was what they thought was the most likely outcome, *median effort* if a time prediction was what they thought was about 50% likely not to be exceeded, and *risk-averse effort* if a time prediction was considered very likely to be sufficient to complete the work.

Table 3.2 What do software developers mean when communicating a time prediction?

Meaning	Percentage of respondents (%)
Ideal effort	37
Most likely effort	27
Median effort	5
Risk-averse effort	9
Don't know	22

In spite of the same time prediction instructions and the same prediction task, the meanings of the predictions differed greatly (see Table 3.2). In addition, a large proportion of the software developers, all of whom regularly produced and communicated time predictions, openly admitted that they did not really know what they meant by their time predictions.

We have conducted several studies of this type in various contexts and they all show great variety in what is meant by a time prediction. This was the case even within a homogeneous context, such as within a single company. The studies also confirm that the meaning is usually not communicated by those producing the time prediction and that those receiving the predictions rarely requested such information. Requesting a time prediction without stating precisely what is wanted could lead to time predictions representing anything from *best-case* to *risk-averse* thinking. Much of what seem to be time prediction errors and unrealistic plans may simply be the consequences of poor communication of the meaning of the predictions.

Sometimes people try to explain what their time prediction means by including verbal probabilities or qualifiers, such as '*very likely* to take less than four hours', '*possible* to be completed in two days', '*will* take about three hours', and '*can* take 10 hours'. Such phrases are not only vague with a strongly context-dependent meaning [5], but also frequently misunderstood. The time prediction 'it *can* be finished in five days' is, for example, likely to be understood differently by the person communicating it and the person receiving it. The person communicating it tends to think that five days is an *extreme* outcome, in this case, perhaps the best-case outcome. The person who receives the time prediction will, on the other hand, tend to interpret it as a *likely* outcome [6]. While using the word *can* ensures that you are never wrong (you never claimed that it was certain or even likely that the job would be finished in five days), it is certainly not a precise way of communicating time predictions. Similar interpretation challenges accompany the use of *more than* and *less than*. A task predicted to take more than 10 hours may, for example, be interpreted as larger than one predicted to take less than 20 hours [7]. The use of verbal probabilities and qualifiers, in spite of their frequent use in professional and daily life, turns out not to be very helpful when communicating time predictions.

In some cases, we can make a good guess, perhaps based on the context and previous experience, of what is meant by a time prediction. If someone says, 'I'll be there in 5 minutes', our previous experience with that person may tell us that this is a *best-case* time prediction. If nothing goes wrong, the person will be there in five to 15 minutes; otherwise, it may take much more time. In cases in which we have little experience, the lack of explanation of what is meant by a time prediction may be quite unfortunate and lead to frustration and poor decisions. One way to give time predictions more meaning and to communicate that meaning is through the use of probabilities and distributions. This is the topic of the next section.

Take home message 1: It is often not clear what people mean when they give a time prediction. The meaning varies greatly and is sometimes not even clear to those who made the time prediction.

Take home message 2: Not explaining what is meant by a time prediction and not asking for an explanation of its intended meaning may lead to misunderstandings and unrealistic plans.

3.3 Probability-Based Time Predictions

The time usage to complete a task may be predicted and given meaning through the use of a frequency distribution of the actual time usage of similar tasks on previous occasions. Assume, for example, that driving your car to work from home usually takes about 30 minutes. It may take a bit less, a bit more, or much more time if there is a great deal of traffic or an accident blocking the road. Let us say that the frequency distribution of driving times, when starting from home between 8 a.m. and 9 a.m., based on 1000 observations, is as shown in Fig. 3.1.

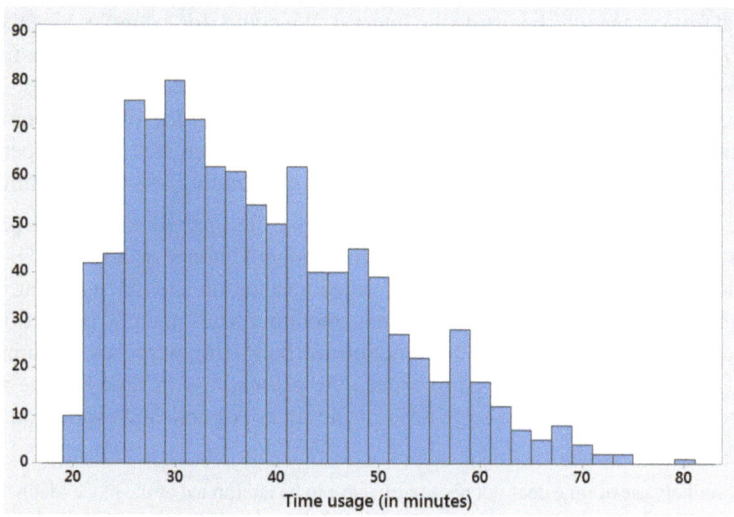

Fig. 3.1 Frequency distribution of driving times between home and work

The distribution in Fig. 3.1 tells us that approximately 30 minutes is the most likely driving time, with 80 observations. This value is called the *mode* in statistics.[1] In many cases, the most likely time usage is good enough as a time prediction. If, on the other hand, we need to be fairly sure of being on time, the most likely time usage may not be very helpful. The distribution in Fig. 3.1 tells us that we will use 30 minutes or less only in about 30% of the times, that is, only 30% of the observations of previous driving times are on the left side of 30 minutes in our distribution. If the past is a reliable indicator of future time usage, this means that it is only 30% likely that 30 minutes will be enough. To be quite sure to be on time, say, 90% sure, we should draw a vertical line in Fig. 3.1 so that 90% of the observations are on the left side. For the distribution in Fig. 3.1, this corresponds to a value of 55 minutes. We would then, for example, have to leave home at 7:05 a.m. to be 90% sure of arriving before 8:00 a.m. To be 99% sure of being on time, we would need an even higher value from the distribution of past time usage. In Fig. 3.1, 99% certainty corresponds to about 70 minutes. In other words, we would have to leave home at 6:50 a.m. to be 99% sure of arriving before 9:00 a.m. The distribution in Fig. 3.1 also illustrates our previous point about how meaningless it can be to talk about a time prediction without stating what it means.

To communicate the meaning of time predictions, we can use probabilities and distributions in several ways:

- We may present the full distribution of possible time outcomes, that is, the full distribution of Fig. 3.1. The receiver of the time prediction may then use the value that best reflects his or her time prediction needs.
- We may present a two-sided time prediction interval. A two-sided time prediction interval is a minimum–maximum interval together with the probability that the actual time usage will be inside the interval. We could, for example, give the 90% prediction interval of 23–60 minutes, because 90% of the observations for past time usage in Fig. 3.1 are more than 23 minutes and less than 60 minutes.
- We may present a one-sided prediction interval. Using the observations in the distribution in Fig. 3.1, we may predict that it is 50% likely that we will spend less than 36 minutes or that we are 90% confident of spending less than 55 minutes.

One-sided prediction intervals are sometimes called *pX predictions*. A pX prediction of Y hours means that we think that using Y hours or less is X% likely. Time usage pX predictions are used for project evaluation and management in several domains. When used for project management purposes, the p50 prediction may be used for planning and the p85 prediction for budgeting purposes, meaning that 50% of projects are not expected to exceed the planned use of time and the budget is expected to be sufficiently large 85% of the time. A published evaluation report

---

[1] The most likely use of time does not necessarily have to be interpreted as the mode (defined as the most frequently observed value) of the empirical distribution. The 'natural peak' of the distribution, if we draw a smooth line over the bins in Fig. 3.1, is what we would consider as the most likely use of time, but this does not necessarily correspond to the most frequently observed value in the data. The most frequently observed value also depends on the granularity of the time usage values included in the distribution (decimals may give a different mode than whole minutes).

suggests that the implementation of these two types of pX predictions and associated uncertainty assessment methods have a positive impact on the realism of project time and cost predictions.[2]

A time prediction can be any value of the outcome distribution as long as we explain what is meant. Three values of the probability distribution are, however, of special interest for time predictions: the mode (the most likely value), the median (the middle observations, or p50 prediction), and the mean (the expected value).

The most likely use of time is usually easy to identify from the distribution, since it is the point or interval with the highest frequency of occurrence. The most likely use of time is the value we would choose if we tried to maximize the *likelihood of very accurate time predictions*. Using the data in Fig. 3.1, we would find that a time prediction based on the most likely value (30 minutes) would be within ±5 minutes of the actual time in 36% of the cases. The corresponding proportion of time predictions within ±5 minutes would be 30% when using the median (38 minutes) as our time prediction and 27% when using the mean (40 minutes). The drawback is that, by maximizing the likelihood of very accurate predictions, we may harm our other time prediction goals. The *median* and *mean* values have properties that often make them more suitable as time prediction values.

The *median use of time* in Fig. 3.1 is 37 minutes. The median is the value we would chose if we were trying to *minimize the mean deviation between the predicted and the actual time usage*. Using the data in Fig. 3.1, we would have a mean time prediction error of nine minutes when using the median as our prediction, 11 minutes when using the most likely time as our prediction, and 10 minutes when using the mean value as our prediction. Although the most likely time usage is more often very accurate, it is sometimes far off, which makes the median more accurate, on average. Another useful property of the median value is that it is frequently more robust than the mean value; that is, it is less affected by extreme values. This is especially useful if we have few observations of past time usage.

The *mean use of time* is the sum of individual time usages divided by the number of observations. The mean value in Fig. 3.1 is about 40 minutes. This value is hard to observe directly from the distribution and frequently hard to judge based on experience, partly because it may be strongly affected by extreme values. The mean is the point in the distribution where the *sum of the time prediction error will be the same for all overruns as it is for all underruns*.[3] This is difficult to imagine, so it may, instead, be useful to think of the mean value as the *balance point* of the distribution. Assume that the distribution in Fig. 3.1 is placed on an old-fashioned scale. The mean value would be the point of the scale where the scale would be in balance, whereas the point of the median or the most likely value would result in imbalance (see Fig. 3.2, where the left panel shows the use of the mean and the right panel the median as the points where we try to balance the scale).

---

[2]See [8]. The report has possible selection bias due to the omission of projects that completely failed, but, even after adjusting for this, there seems to be a positive effect on prediction realism.

[3]The mean value also optimizes the square of the deviations between predicted and actual time usage.

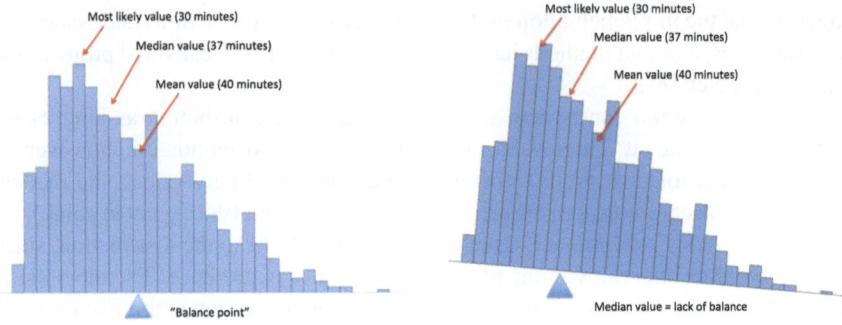

Fig. 3.2 Mode, median, and mean values of a distribution

The mean value takes into account how far away extreme observations are, since a value that is 14 hours more than the balance point has the same weight as 14 values that are one hour less than the balance point. In contrast, to find the median value, one just has to count the observations and ensure that *as many observations are above as below it*. Research suggests that we tend to underestimate the mean value when presented with a right-skewed distribution, such as the distribution in Fig. 3.1 [9], and when establishing the distribution from memory.

If the mode and the median are easier to understand and to calculate and are more robust (less affected by outliers) than the mean, why do we want to determine the mean of an outcome distribution? The main reason for using the mean when predicting time is that the mean value minimizes the deviation between the sum of time predictions and the sum of the actual time usages. When we want to know the total time usage of a set of tasks or projects, that is, when we want to add time predictions, this property is crucial. It may be required, for example, when breaking down a project and summarizing time predictions of subtasks or when considering the overall potential for cost overrun of a set of projects.

If, for example, we use the prediction of the most likely time usage to predict driving to work from home 10 times, the sum of these predictions is likely be too low to reflect the actual total time. If, on the other hand, we use the mean prediction, we would typically be more correct about the total time of driving 10 times. Similarly, if you are the chief executive officer of a large company and have four large projects running with *most likely* costs of $500 million each, you should not expect the total costs to be $2 billion but, most likely, substantially higher, given the right-skewness of most project cost distributions. We explain in more detail about why this is so and how to properly add time predictions later in this book. Table 3.3 summarizes the suitability of the most likely, median, and mean time prediction values, given different time prediction goals.

You may have started wondering how we can know the time usage distributions, which is a prerequisite for even thinking about using the mode, median, and mean time usage as our time prediction. In some cases, we have highly relevant data about past time usage, perhaps for travel times or production times enabling such

Table 3.3 The suitability of the prediction type depends on the prediction goal

Type of prediction	Time prediction accuracy goal		
	High likelihood of a very accurate time prediction	Low expected difference between predicted and actual time usage	Low difference between the sum of time predictions and the sum of actual time usage
Most likely outcome	++	–	–
Median outcome	+	++	+
Mean outcome	–	+	++

Note ++good, +acceptable, –do not use

knowledge, as in Fig. 3.1. More often, this is not the case. Since we hardly ever know the exact probabilities of future outcomes, we may have to try to derive or guess the outcome distribution from memory and other knowledge, that is, by expert judgement. Although sometimes hard, this approach is required to provide a good model for thinking and talking about time predictions, to enable us to connect prediction goals with types of time predictions, and to be precise about the uncertainty of our time predictions. You can read more about how to derive time usage distributions in Chap. 6.

Take home message 1: Good ways of presenting and communicating your time predictions include those using two-sided prediction intervals, such as 'it is X% likely that the work will take between Y and Z hours', and those using one-sided prediction intervals (pX predictions), such as 'I am X% confident that it will take less than Y hours'.

Take home message 2: Different values of the outcome distribution, such as the most likely, the median, and the mean, optimize different time prediction accuracy functions and meet different time prediction goals.

3.4   Right-Skewed Time Distributions

As part of his work as a graphic designer, Tom is asked to take photos of trees, flowers, and people for use in digital illustrations. The last time he went to take photos for a similar project, he spent about five hours. He is aware that the time usage may vary from occasion to occasion, so he tells his manager that he expects to be back in five hours plus or minus two hours. What is wrong with Tom's time prediction?

There may be several questionable elements of Tom's time predictions, such as not communicating how likely he believes that the actual time will be within the stated interval, but the problem we are concerned with in this section is his idea of a *symmetric* interval, or symmetric distribution, of time usage. Although we do not

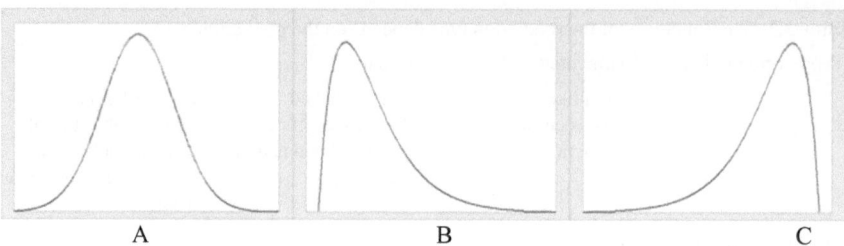

A   B   C

Fig. 3.3 Symmetric, right-skewed, and left-skewed distributions

really know what is going on in Tom's mind, it seems as if he assumes that two hours more than the predicted time is as likely as two hours less. If Tom were aware of the typical asymmetric distribution of time usage, he should have given an *asymmetric* interval. An asymmetric and probably more realistic time prediction could be, for example, that the shoot *will most likely take about five hours, most certainly between four and eight hours*.

Maybe the only data of past time usage Tom could think of concerned the last time he did a similar project, so he is excused for not considering the entire distribution of potential time usage. However, let us say that there are a few hundred graphic designers such as Tom, all performing the same or highly similar tasks, and that we plot all their actual time usages for this task in a graph. What would this look like? In Fig. 3.3, we present three different alternatives.

The distribution in panel A is a symmetric, so-called normal, or Gaussian, distribution, where spending one hour more than the most likely time usage is just as likely as spending one hour less. Distribution A corresponds to Tom's naïve belief about time usage when giving a time usage interval symmetric around the most likely value. The distribution in panel B is right-skewed, that is, a distribution with a long right tail. Distribution B would be the result if a task is as likely to take a bit less as it is to take a lot longer than usual. Distribution C is left-skewed, that is, a distribution with a long left tail. It would be the result if a task is as likely to take substantially less as it is to take slightly more than usual. Which figure is likely to correspond to the distribution of time usage for a few hundred graphic designers doing the same task?

Most time usage distributions seem to be most similar to distribution B. Time usage distributions tend to have a long and sometimes thick right tail. The thickness and length of the tail may vary, but we have yet to see a time usage distribution that is strongly left-skewed, such as distribution C in Fig. 3.3. We therefore feel quite confident about claiming that nearly all time usage distributions are right-skewed. Why is this so and why is it relevant?

Right-skewed distributions are found everywhere in nature. They are probably more common than symmetric ones and could be the result of a range of different processes.[4] In the realm of time usage, right-skewed distributions may be related to the fact that no activity can take less than zero time to complete, while there is hardly any absolute upper time limit for any activity. Even the slightest activity, given terrible luck or extreme perfectionism, can take a very long time. The poet Franz Wright spent six years on a five-line poem [11]—but no poem has ever been written in zero seconds or less.

Related to the lack of an upper boundary of time usage, you may have experienced that more things can go *very wrong* than *very right*. The history of the Sagrada Familia cathedral is a good example of how bad things can go. Construction began in 1883, was only 15% completed in 1926, and was predicted in 2013 to be finished in 2026. Among other events, delays were caused by inconsistent funding, a civil war, two world wars, highly complex construction work, and a change of architects. There is no shortage of projects or endeavours similar to this one, where the list of possible negative events leading to greater time usage is nearly endless [12].

What about projects that are extremely successful? Of course, there are projects completed ahead of their time predictions and with lower costs than predicted. For instance, the T-REX infrastructure project in Denver finished 22 months ahead of schedule, which is rather substantial for a project predicted to last about seven years. Doing things in new and clever ways and the use of new technology may decrease duration and costs somewhat, but we have yet to see a project predicted to last five years taking two weeks or a project predicted to cost $2 billion ending up with costs of about $1000. Thus, there is a limit on how fast one can do something and how inexpensive projects turn out to be, but hardly any limit to the other end of the scale. Furthermore, we rarely plan our projects to be inefficient, so our predictions are often based on imagining success [13], which also limits the potential for completing projects ahead of schedule and with less time usage than predicted.

There is also another, frequently forgotten reason why the distributions of time usages is right-skewed. Consider a run on a 400-metre track under windy conditions. In one of the straight 100-metre sections, there is a headwind, decreasing the speed, and in the other a tailwind, increasing the speed. One could easily think that the negative effect of headwind is compensated for by the positive effect of tailwind. The hindrance (the headwind), however, *lasts longer* (in spite of the same distance) than the advantage (the tailwind), leading to a slower total time compared to a situation without wind. While this may seem like a strange example, it illustrates an effect that may contribute to right-skewed distributions of task completion time: An increase in time usage in a project due to negative events enables more negative events to happen due to more time spent, which generates further increases in time usage and greater right-skewness (which enables even more negative events to happen and so on). The Sagrada Familia construction is such an example. The initial delays enabled further delays due to the civil war and two world wars. In contrast, a project's high

---

[4]See [10]. This paper argues against the use of the central limit theory to claim the dominance of normal distributions in nature. Observed distributions are the result of several combinatory processes, not just the addition of independent elements, which is a prerequisite for the generation of a normal distribution.

productivity is not likely to be a factor contributing to a higher likelihood of even further increases in productivity. If anything, high productivity reduces opportunities for further decreases in time usage because there is less time left to be shortened.

Take home message 1: Based on empirical data and on analytical reasoning we can assume that typical distributions of time usages are right-skewed, that is, have a longer tail towards higher values.

Take home message 2: The most extreme deviations from typical time usage are nearly always found on the right side of the distribution. That is, one can use much longer times than what is common or expected, but one rarely experiences extreme cases of using less. In any case, the lower limit of time usage is zero.

Take home message 3: The hours saved from times you are more productive than usual (e.g. tailwind) will seldom compensate for the hours lost from times you are less productive than usual (e.g. headwind). In other words, your efficiency is rarely as extreme as your inefficiency.

3.5   Relearning to Add: 2 + 2 Is Usually More Than 4

Most people think they know how to add. It may therefore come as a surprise that, in the world of time predictions, 2 hours + 2 hours is often not 4 hours. It is usually *more* than 4 hours, perhaps as much as 5 or 6 hours. The nonintuitive addition of time predictions is a consequence of the probabilistic (stochastic) nature of time usage and its right-skewed distribution.

To illustrate what happens if we add time predictions the way we learned in school, we reuse the example of driving to work from home. If you do not recall it, have another look at Fig. 3.1 (Sect. 3.3). The figure shows the distribution of time usage of a drive to work from home. What do you think is the most likely *total* usage of time for one full year of driving, assuming that we drive 200 times per year?

If we add all the most likely values for each of the 200 trips (=30 minutes × 200), the most likely total time usage for one year would be predicted to be 6000 minutes (=100 hours). This prediction of the total time usage would be far too low to reflect the likely total time usage.

Assume that we sample 200 outcomes from the distribution in Fig. 3.1 and sum them. This simulates the total driving time for one year. If we repeat this sampling process 1000 times, we obtain a distribution of the total time for one year of driving based on 1000 values. One such distribution is displayed in Fig. 3.4. As can be seen, a prediction of 6000 minutes based on summing the most likely time usages is not even close to the lowest observed sum of the time usage. The most likely sum of time usage is, instead, somewhere around 8000 minutes. What is going on? Why is the sum of the most likely time usages not the most likely sum of time usage? (If you find this question difficult to grasp, you are not alone).

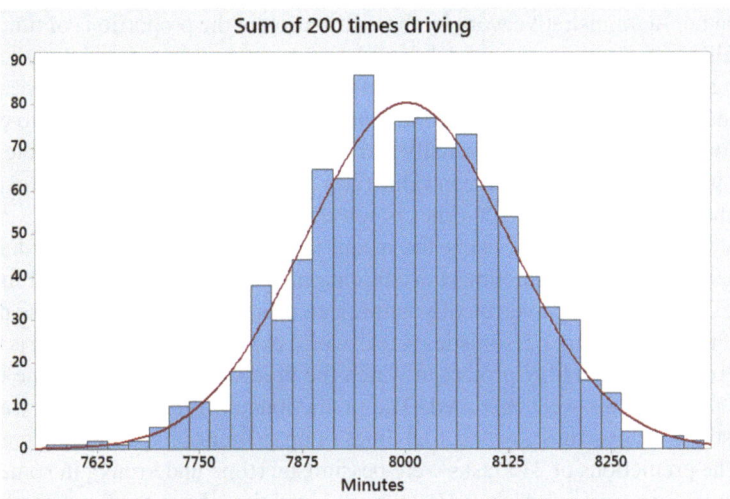

Fig. 3.4 Frequency distribution of total time usage from driving 200 times

To correctly add time predictions, we need to take the long tail of the distribution of driving time usage into account. In that respect, the *most likely* time predictions do a poor job. So does the median value. In the case of the 200 trips from home to work, adding the median predictions would yield a total prediction of 7400 minutes (the median of 37 minutes multiplied by 200 trips = 7400 minutes). As can be seen in Fig. 3.4, this prediction is also far too low to be realistic. The only type of prediction that can be used here is predictions of the *mean* driving time. In contrast to the median and the most likely values, the mean value incorporates the extreme values of the long tail of the distribution.

Adding the mean values also leads to some statistical magic. Even if the individual time usage distributions are heavily skewed (as in Fig. 3.1), the distributions of the total time (as in Fig. 3.4) will approach symmetry and consequently have similar values for the most likely, median, and mean total time usage values. This magic is described as the *central limit theorem* from statistical theory, which holds that the sums of distributions, even heavily skewed ones, will be close to a normal, symmetric distribution if certain conditions are met, such as independence of the added elements. To be honest, this magic rarely represents the time usage outcome distribution in real-life projects. There are usually numerous dependencies between tasks and tasks that are forgotten in the time predictions, leading to a right-skewed outcome distribution of the sum. A common example of dependency between tasks is when the time spent on one activity is a proportion of another, that is, there is multiplicative dependency between tasks. Take, for example, the common situation in projects in which the time spent on administration is a proportion of the time spent on construction work. If the time spent on construction increases, so does the time spent on administration. To find the time spent on administration, we may either multiply the distribution of time spent on non-administrative work by the distribution of the proportions of time spent on administration, or we can model the relation by including a correlation between the two activities.[5] Back in our example of driving, where we assume independence of the individual driving times, the *total time usage* of 200 trips from home to work is likely to be an approximately normally and symmetrically distributed variable with a central value of 200 times the mean value (200×40 minutes = 8000).[6] The expected total time usage for driving 200 times is consequently 8000 minutes.

The differences between using the mean, the most likely, and the median values when adding time predictions have fascinating practical implications. First, you might experience a time overrun of your project, even when most of the time predictions of the subtasks are pessimistic. A real-world example of this situation is that of an information technology project in which the predictions and actual time usages of 443 project tasks were recorded. The predictions of 196 of the tasks were too optimistic (time overruns), with actual times of up to four or five times the predicted time. The predictions of 215 tasks were pessimistic (time underruns), in some cases with actual time usages less than 1/10 the predicted time. In spite of more tasks with pessimistic predictions than optimistic predictions, there was a time overrun for the project at large. The predicted number of work hours spent on the 443 tasks was 2723, whereas the actual number of work hours on the same tasks was 3130 (15% overrun).[7] Overpessimism at the task level and overoptimism at the aggregated project level is perfectly understandable when taking the long, fat tail of time distributions into account. If you predict that a task will take 30 hours and it takes 10 times as long, you have a 270-hour overrun. If you manage to spend only 1/10 of the predicted time, you have a time underrun of only 27 hours. Cases of underrun rarely compensate for cases of overrun. Inefficiency trumps efficiency.

We frequently have an interest in the total time usage. We may, for example, have many smaller tasks to complete at home and wonder if we are able to manage them all. Companies may have several projects running simultaneously and are interested in the total cost compared to the total budget, and most projects include numerous subtasks. If we want to take control over our schedules and investments, we have to take the challenge of adding time predictions seriously. It is likely that many time overruns are caused not by poor time prediction abilities but, rather, by poor time prediction *addition* abilities.

---

[5] All too often, as far as we have experienced, time predictions are added, for example, using Monte Carlo simulation, without modelling the dependencies between the elements. This results in an unrealistic symmetric distribution of total time usage, in accordance with the central limit theorem. We strongly recommend modelling the main dependencies when predicting the time usage of larger projects. Use for example the free risk analysis tool Riscue (www.riscue.com), or commercial tools such as @RISK (www.palisade.com/risk/) for this purpose.

[6] In this case, but not generally, it is reasonable to assume independence between the added element (the driving times), implying that the central limit theorem creates the magic and the distribution becomes symmetric. When a distribution is symmetric, the mode, median, and the mean—that is, the central values—are the same.

[7] A perhaps even better demonstration of this counterintuitive outcome comes from a study of 4000 software projects. In this study, overestimation was just as common as underestimation (with a median time overrun of around 0%), but the mean time overrun was as high as 107%. See [14].

Take home message 1: The sum of the most likely time usages of individual activities is not the same as the most likely total time usage of the same activities. When adding most likely time predictions, you will obtain a prediction of the most likely total time usage that is too low.

Take home message 2: For the proper addition of time predictions, you should add the predicted *mean* value of each subtask.

3.6 How to Predict the Mean Time Usage

The previous section demonstrated that predictions of the most likely time usage of tasks cannot be added to obtain the expected total time usage. For this purpose, we need predictions of the mean time usage of all subtasks. Unfortunately, it is not likely that you will receive the predicted mean time usage even when explicitly requested. Determination of the mean value is much more complex than finding the middle (median) or most frequent (most likely, mode) value of a distribution. Even when you observe the full distribution of past outcomes, it may be difficult to judge what is the mean value.

One common approach to obtain predictions of the mean value is to derive a distribution based on so-called three-point estimation. The Program Evaluation and Review Technique (PERT) project planning approach, for example, requires the input of the most likely value, the minimum (best-case) value, and the maximum (worst-case) value [15] and calculates the mean by use of the formula

$$Mean = \frac{minimum + 4 \cdot most\ likely + maximum}{6}$$

The PERT method and similar approaches may be helpful in solving the problem of finding the mean value but they introduce new ones. One problem is that people are typically very poor at making best- and worst-case time usage predictions. For instance, in one study, students first predicted the time usage they were 99% sure not to exceed (the p99 prediction) for software development tasks, along with the best case that would occur with only a 1% chance (the p1 prediction). This means that, in 98% of the cases (=p99 − p1), given realistic values, the actual time usage should be between the stated minimum and maximum time usages. This did not happen. After completing the tasks, it turned out that the actual time usage was inside their 98% confidence intervals in only 57% of the cases [16]. This result is typical of studies where people are asked to give minimum and maximum values (see Chap. 6 for more on this issue). To make things even worse, the original PERT approach assumes that the best- and worst-case predictions respectively correspond to p0 and p100,[8] which,

---

[8]That is, the value that is so low it has a 0% probability of occurring and the value of which you are 100% not to exceed. Note that there are modifications of the PERT model that enable the use of p10 and p90 instead of p0 and p100, such as described in [17].

for most real-world tasks, are meaningless values that are impossible to derive from experience or historical data.

As an alternative to the current approaches, such as the PERT model, we developed a new three-point prediction tool (a spreadsheet model) that provides predictions of mean outcomes based on user-determined confidence levels.[9] We believe that the tool has several important features that make it different from and perhaps better than other approaches. First, it forces the person making the prediction to look back and use historical information. Neglecting historical information may be one of the main reasons for poor time usage predictions in many domains [18]. Second, the tool does not require the prediction of extreme outcomes, such p1 or p95 predictions. Third, it does not require a particular meaning of the time prediction used as reference (median, most likely, p85, etc.), as long as the meaning is the same used for previous time predictions. The steps to calculate the mean time prediction are as follows:

1. *Predict the time usage.* The prediction, the reference, may be a prediction of the most likely use of time or any other type of time prediction.
2. *Assess the accuracy of similar past predictions.* Select two prediction accuracy points for which you have historical information or can make a qualified judgement. Each accuracy point should include (a) the prediction error (the deviation of actual outcomes from the prediction) and (b) the frequency of occurrence. For example, you may know that, for about seven out of 10 (70% occurrence) previously completed tasks similar to the one being predicted, you spent less than 130% of the predicted time. This means that your p70 prediction is 130%. You need one more such accuracy point. The second assessment could, for example, be that you spent less than 90% of the predicted time in three out of 10 cases (30% occurrence), meaning that your p30 prediction is 90%.
3. *Input the accuracy points into the spreadsheet*, which calculates the uncertainty distribution, the pX values and the mean value.

Example: Assume that you have predicted the most likely time usage to be 30 minutes. You know from similar situations that, in about 90% of the cases, the actual time usage was less than twice (200%) your predicted time usage and that, in about 50% of the cases, the actual time usage was less than 130% of your predicted time usage. This means that you have a p90 prediction of 200% the original prediction and a p50 prediction of 130% the original prediction. Using the spreadsheet, assuming a lognormal distribution of time usage,[10] yields a mean time prediction of 41 minutes. The time usage distribution is displayed in Fig. 3.5, showing, for example, that the most likely value is around 33 minutes. The pX distribution is displayed in Fig. 3.6, showing, for instance, that the p95 prediction is a bit less than 70 minutes. For more details on this method for making realistic pX predictions, including more examples, see Chap. 6.

---

[9]Downloadable from www.simula.no/~magnej/Time_predictions_book.

[10]It is possible to extend the spreadsheet to distributions, but lognormal distributions seems to accommodate most of the typical time usage distributions.

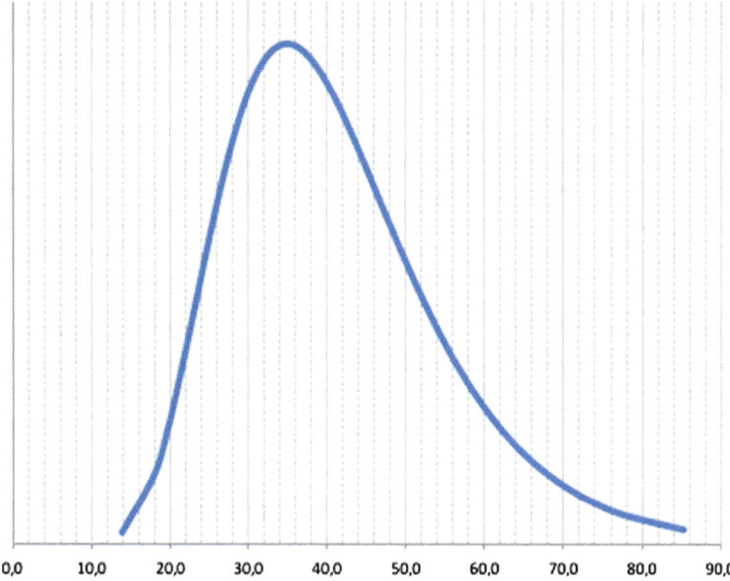

Fig. 3.5 Time usage distribution (density)

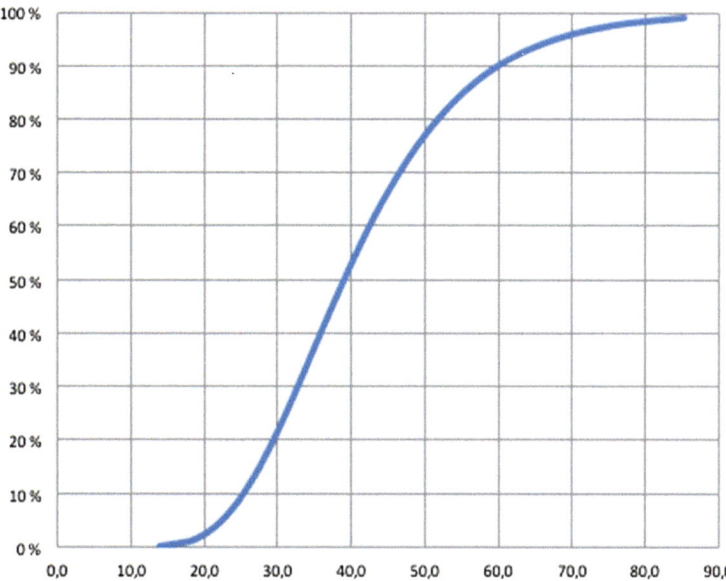

Fig. 3.6 A pX distribution (cumulative probability distribution) of time usage

Take home message 1: The calculations of the predicted mean value of an outcome distribution are typically based on giving two or three points, such as a low value, the most likely value, and a high value, of the distribution as input.

Take home message 2: Predictions of a low value (e.g. a p10 prediction) and a high value (e.g. a p90 prediction), when unaided by historical data and proper methods, tend to be very inaccurate and result in underestimation of the time usage uncertainty. Methods that do not compensate for this human bias, such as typical use of the PERT method, will tend to underestimate the mean values and, consequently, the total time usage.

Take home message 3: This book offers a method and a tool for predicting the mean value from two user-determined points of the historical time prediction error distribution.

3.7   How Time Predictions Affect Performance

Predicting the weather does not have any effect on the actual weather. Predicting time usage is different, since the prediction can have an impact on the actual time usage [19]. A famous book by Parkinson, the fellow behind the 'law' stating that work expands to fill the time available for its completion, includes a story that nicely illustrates this difference [20]. The story is about an elderly lady who spends a whole day to send a postcard to her niece. First, she has to go buy the postcard, then she must walk home and find her glasses, decide on what to write, write it, eat lunch, decide on whether to take an umbrella or not, buy stamps, drink another cup of tea, and so forth. The lady's prediction of the time it takes to send a postcard would be a full day, because she has a full day available. A busy lady would perhaps predict spending five minutes on the same task, because that is all the time she has available. An extension of Parkinson's law, relevant in many contexts, would be that many types of work expands to fill the time available for its completion, plus a little more. Even with plenty of time to complete a task, we may end up with a time overrun due to low productivity in the initial stages or poor planning of the time required for the last part of the job. The old lady may, for example, receive a visitor just before she is going to post the postcard in the afternoon, miss the hours the post office is open, and have to postpone the rest of the task to the next day.

If too high time predictions can lead to lower productivity, what about too low time predictions? Do they lead to increased productivity? A study on software development teams found an inverted U-shaped relation between the degree of perceived time pressure and productivity [21]. Here, time pressure was measured as how much the team's initial time predictions were reduced based on pressure (negotiation) from the client.[11] The study found that, if the software development teams were allowed

---

[11] More precisely, they measured time pressure as (*time predicted by the development team—time negotiated by the customer*)/*time predicted by the development team*.

Fig. 3.7 Possible effect of
time pressure on productivity

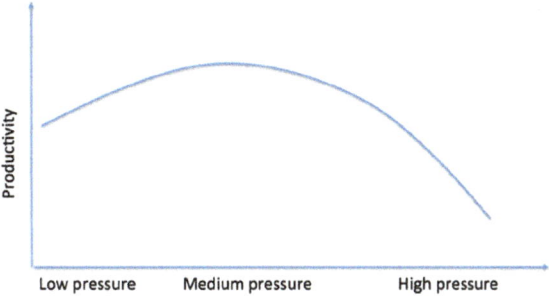

Fig. 3.8 Possible effect of
time pressure on quality

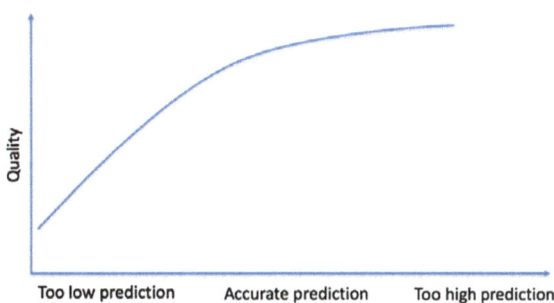

to use their original time predictions as the planned time, they had lower productivity than when the time predictions were reduced by up to 20% due to client negotiations. However, when the reduction in planned time continued beyond 20%, the time pressure became too high and productivity tended to decline. Figure 3.7 illustrates a possible relation between time pressure and productivity.

Other contexts may show different results as to when pressure is positive and negative, but it is reasonable to believe that, in many contexts, a great deal of time pressure and very little time pressure both have negative consequences on productivity.

Not only can work productivity be affected by pressure from low time predictions, but also the quality of the work. In an experiment, we found an increase in the number of errors made by software programmers when the time prediction was intentionally set 40% below what we would expect from the participants' previous work [22]. Based on that study and other experience, the relation between time prediction-induced work pressure and quality could be as depicted in Fig. 3.8.

Since time predictions can affect quality and productivity, the introduction of incentives, such as evaluations or financial rewards, to achieve time prediction accuracy can be problematic, as the following real-world example illustrates.

A company introduced a financial bonus for those project leaders who made accurate project time usage predictions. The following year, time prediction accuracy improved greatly, but the company also experienced a decrease in productivity. What happened was a natural reaction to the new practice of rewarding accurate time predictions. Project managers, smart as they are, raised their time usage predictions to predictions they were almost certain not to exceed. The extra buffer in the planned use of effort was used for improvements in quality, training, testing, and documentation (exploiting Parkinson's law). For the company, this decrease in productivity was not beneficial and it soon stopped rewarding accurate time predictions.

The strategies of producing accurate time predictions by lowering productivity in situations with too high time predictions or cutting corners in situations with too low time predictions require the work process or product to be flexible. This is the case for much of what we do in life. If I make a bet on how long it will take to drive to work, I may be able to win the bet by adjusting my behaviour, especially if the prediction is high. If my prediction is as long as 60 minutes, I can drive slowly, stop at the gas station to fill up the tank, and spend time on searching for the perfect parking spot. If my prediction is a bit on the low side, for example, 25 minutes, I can drive fast, violate traffic rules, and park illegally. We could call the first prediction accuracy strategy work stretching (stretching work to fit a high prediction) and the second work shrinking (shrinking work to fit a low prediction). These strategies are common. Without them, our time predictions would look worse—sometimes much worse—than they currently do. Stretching and shrinking may sometimes be acceptable, but these strategies may violate other important goals, such as productivity and quality.

Take home message 1: Time predictions may affect the work, especially when it is highly flexible. Time predictions that are slightly too low may increase productivity, while those that are much too low or too high may decrease productivity. Time predictions that are too low may also lead to reductions in the quality of the work.

Take home message 2: Rewarding accurate time predictions is usually not a good idea, particularly if people behave strategically and stretch the work (lower work productivity) or shrink it (lower work quality) to fit the prediction.[12]

References

1. Jørgensen M, Teigen KH (2002) Uncertainty intervals versus interval uncertainty: an alternative method for eliciting effort prediction intervals in software development projects. In: International conference on project management (ProMAC). Singapore, pp 343–352
2. Teigen KH (1990) To be convincing or to be right: a question of preciseness. In: Gilhooly KJ, Keane MTG, Logie RH, Erdös G (eds) Lines of thinking. Wiley, Chichester, pp 299–313
3. Jørgensen M (2016) The use of precision of software development effort estimates to communicate uncertainty. In: International conference on software quality. Springer International Publishing, pp 156–168
4. Jørgensen M (2014) Communication of software cost estimates. In: Proceedings of the 18th international conference on evaluation and assessment in software engineering, ACM, p 28

---

[12]The second strategy may be meaningful within a framework of a fixed budget and flexible content (design to cost, agile development with flexible scope, etc.). In that case, the pressure is not necessarily to reduce the quality, given insufficient time to complete all the tasks but, rather, to reduce the amount of deliveries.

5. Brun W, Teigen KH (1988) Verbal probabilities: ambiguous, context-dependent, or both? Organ Behav Hum Decis Process 41(3):390–404
6. Teigen KH, Filkuková P (2013) Can > will: predictions of what can happen are extreme, but believed to be probable. J Behav Decis Making 26(1):68–78
7. Teigen KH, Halberg AM, Fostervold KI (2007) Single-limit interval estimates as reference points. Appl Cogn Psychol 21(3):383–406
8. Samset K, Volden GH (2013) Investing for impact. Concept report 36. www.ntnu.no/documents/1261860271/1262010703/Concept_rapport_nr_36.pdf. Accessed March 2017
9. Peterson C, Miller A (1964) Mode, median, and mean as optimal strategies. J Exp Psychol 68(4):363
10. Limpert E, Stahel WA, Abbt M (2001) Log-normal distributions across the sciences: keys and clues. Bioscience 51(5):341–352
11. Hilbert E (2006) The secret glory. An interview with Franz Wright. See www.cprw.com/Hilbert/wright.htm. Accessed March 2017
12. Silverman J, Kiger PJ 10 construction projects that broke the bank. science.howstuffworks.com/engineering/structural/10-construction-projects.htm#page=5. Accessed March 2017
13. Newby-Clark IR, Ross M, Buehler R, Koehler DJ, Griffin D (2000) People focus on optimistic scenarios and disregard pessimistic scenarios while predicting task completion times. J Exp Psychol: Appl 6(3):171–182
14. Budzier A, Flyvbjerg B (2013) Making sense of the impact and importance of outliers in project management through the use of power laws. In: Proceedings of IRNOP (International Research Network on Organizing by Projects)
15. Wikipedia: The free encyclopedia program evaluation and review technique. en.wikipedia.org/wiki/Program_evaluation_and_review_technique. Accessed March 2017
16. Connolly T, Dean D (1997) Decomposed versus holistic estimates of effort required for software writing tasks. Manag Sci 43(7):1029–1045
17. Kim SD, Hammond RK, Bickel JE (2014) Improved mean and variance estimating formulas for PERT analyses. IEEE Trans Eng Manag 61(2):362–369
18. Tversky A, Kahneman D (1974) Judgment under uncertainty: heuristics and biases. Science 185(4157):1124–1131
19. Buehler R, Peetz J, Griffin D (2010) Finishing on time: when do predictions influence completion times? Organ Behav Hum Decis Process 111(1):23–32
20. Parkinson CN (1957) Parkinson's law and other studies in administration, vol 24. Houghton Mifflin, Boston
21. Nan N, Harter DE (2009) Impact of budget and schedule pressure on software development cycle time and effort. IEEE Trans Softw Eng 35(5):624–637
22. Jørgensen M, Sjøberg DI (2004) The impact of customer expectation on software development effort estimates. Int J Proj Manag 22(4):317–325

Chapter 4
Overoptimistic Predictions

4.1 Optimism, Overoptimism, and Overoptimistic Predictions

We usually say that a time prediction is overoptimistic when the actual time usage is greater than the predicted time usage. This does not mean that an optimistic or overoptimistic view on time usage was the cause of the too low time prediction. Lack of knowledge, miscalculation during the prediction process, and bad luck in the execution of the project are examples of alternative reasons for too low time predictions. Describing too low, or overoptimistic, time predictions as caused by overoptimism, in the rose-coloured glasses sense, not only is incorrect but may also stop us from seeking other explanations of time overrun besides overoptimism [1].

To clarify the differences between being optimistic or overoptimistic and making optimistic time predictions, let us start by looking into the concepts of optimism and overoptimism. The Oxford English Dictionary describes optimism as 'hopefulness and confidence about the future or the success of something' [2]. If optimism is expecting things to go well, which they sometimes do, we may use the word *overoptimism* when the expected positive outcome is unwarranted, for instance, due to thinking too highly about one's own skill and likelihood of success. If Patricia is an average chess player but rates her chess skill too highly and predicts that she will win a chess tournament where she is far from the best player, she is overoptimistic. Even if it is very unlikely that Patricia will earn first place in the tournament, it is still possible that she will be extremely lucky and win and, consequently, gave a correct prediction. Overoptimism, as we use the term here, does not always lead to overoptimistic predictions.

People tend to be overoptimistic about many things. Married people predict a too low likelihood of getting divorced, car drivers think too highly of their driving skills, and students tend to believe they will obtain better grades on exams than they

© The Author(s) 2018
T. Halkjelsvik and M. Jørgensen, *Time Predictions*, Simula SpringerBriefs on Computing 5, https://doi.org/10.1007/978-3-319-74953-2_4

actually receive.[1] A typical finding is that most people regard themselves as better than average, particularly in completing relatively simple tasks and tasks where they have exceeded a minimum skill level. This phenomenon has been named the *better-than-average effect* and may be seen as a type of overoptimism. The better-than-average type of overoptimism can be illustrated by the perceived likelihood of company success. Entrepreneurs have a high probability of failure and earn, on average, 35% less than employees in similar jobs after 10 years in business [4]. They take a huge risk by investing their own and perhaps even their family members' money and time on something they should know has a high probability of failure. However, if their visions come true, they may have created a new Google or Tesla and contributed to their own and their country's wealth. What is a seemingly unwise decision at the individual level supported by a strong degree of overoptimism may not only be beneficial but also essential for society at large. Had the entrepreneurs been realistic about the amount of time to be spent and the true likelihood of success, they may not have started their companies in the first place.

Overoptimism may be present not only when evaluating our own abilities and opportunities but also when assessing those of people we like. American football supporters consistently predicted, over a period of 17 weeks, that their football team would win more often than they did, even when they could earn money from making more accurate predictions. The predictions made at the end of the season were just as overoptimistic as those at the beginning of the season, despite repeated feedback about actual outcomes [5].

To make the use of optimism-related terms even more confusing, optimism and overoptimism are related to but are not the same as the *personality trait* named optimism. This type of optimism is often described as the tendency to believe that one will generally experience good outcomes in life [6]. Such an optimistic life orientation is associated with a range of beneficial outcomes: a longer life, better recovery from disease, and extended survival times for cancer and AIDS patients [7]. Surprisingly, at least to us, the personality trait of optimism seems to be only weakly, if at all, related to overoptimistic predictions [8], including time predictions [9].

In short, there is more to optimism than overoptimistic time predictions and optimism is far from the only way to explain overoptimistic time predictions. People's desire for success or motivation for a given outcome may produce overoptimistic predictions, but overoptimistic predictions may also be caused by other factors. In the following sections, we will describe in more detail potential causes of and variables related to overoptimistic time predictions.

Take home message: Optimism (i.e. hopefulness for a desired outcome), overoptimism (i.e. unwarranted confidence in a desired outcome), and trait optimism (a personality characteristic related to a positive view of life outcomes) are different aspects of what we typically call optimism. Optimism and overoptimism but not so

---

[1]The grade overoptimism of students is greatest at the beginning of the semester. Just before an exam, when not much more preparation is possible, students tend to give overpessimistic predictions. Then, the motivational effect of grade prediction is no longer there and the prediction may instead be influenced by a wish to prevent disappointment. See [3].

much the trait of optimism may lead to overoptimistic time predictions (i.e., too low predictions), but there are numerous other possible reasons for overoptimistic time predictions.

4.2 The Benefits of Overoptimism

At first glance, it is hard to see how our ancestors, Stone Age humans, would have benefitted from being systematically overoptimistic about time usage or underestimating the risk of actions. Underestimating the consequences of fighting with a person from another tribe or how much effort hunting on the other side of the mountain will require may, for example, lead to an early death or a food shortage. New generations would then be more likely to have the genes of more realistic Stone Age humans able to predict time and risk accurately. However, it seems that many of us are descendants of overoptimistic Stone Age humans. Could it be that overoptimism is rational and adaptive?

In a classic set of experiments from the 1970s, students were repeatedly given the choice to press or not to press a button within a time frame of three seconds [10]. Pressing the button could have the outcome of a light being switched on or the outcome that nothing happened. The light could also switch on if the student chose not to press the button. After 40 trials of button pressing, the participants were asked how much control they thought they had over the light. Even in the experimental situation in which they had absolutely no control of the light switching on or off, the typical student ended up believing that he or she exerted a substantial amount of control, as long as the light was switched on frequently. Typically, the perceived amount of control, when there was no control, was believed to be about 40% on a scale from zero to 100%. Depressed students seemed to be the only group of individuals who were reasonably accurate in their assessment of their influence over the light.

This study was the beginning of research on so-called *depressive realism*. Depressed people seemed to be more realistic than other people, who were generally overoptimistic regarding their influence, their recollection of feedback, their chances of success, and their stance on positive attributes in comparison with others. Unfortunately, as with many other spectacular 'facts' from science, the effect of depression on realism turned out to be very small when all relevant studies were summarized in a meta-analysis [11]. Nevertheless, even a small effect illustrates that optimistic beliefs and predictions may be associated with positive things in life, such as being less depressed. This is further illustrated by studies reporting that unrealistic optimism, or so-called positive illusions, may be good for your mental health [12].

It is even possible that strong overoptimism has helped us survive and reproduce [13]. Assume a very small chance of success for some effortful action, for example, an attempt to make a new, efficient type of weapon that would make hunting easier. Each separate choice of *not* engaging in this action may seem like a good decision, assuming that success is very unlikely and costly in terms of effort and materials. One day, however, someone will succeed in making a better tool or weapon and this is likely to be one of those overoptimistic persons pursuing the near impossible. Now the optimists, or at least one of them, have an advantage in the battle of survival.

Similarly, if all the costs, efforts, delays, and frustrations of a company's ambitious projects were known beforehand, the projects might perhaps never have been initiated. When completed, most of the ambitious projects may have become complete failures, but perhaps one of them became a great success, giving the company a tremendous advantage that more than compensated for all the failures. Preceding many great successes are usually a high number of failures with strongly overoptimistic cost–benefit predictions.

The economist Albert O. Hirschman proposed an argument in favour of being overoptimistic [14]. He argued that people tend to underestimate their creativity and ability to find solutions to problems that emerge. Overoptimistic time and cost predictions may compensate for this overpessimism. Thus, overoptimism is the *hiding hand* that helps us conceal difficulties and encourages us to complete worthwhile projects that we never would have initiated had we known how problematic they would become.

The researchers Flyvbjerg and Sunstein [15] showed that in most large infrastructure projects, difficulties were indeed underestimated, as evident by the strong tendency to experience cost overruns. The benefits, for example, in terms of the number of users of a service, were, on the other hand, typically overestimated. If we overestimate benefits and underestimate costs, we may tend to start projects that are not worthwhile, and the hiding hand will not be as helpful as Hirschman assumed. Flyvbjerg and Sunstein claimed that the negative hiding hand, which they termed the *malevolent hiding hand*, applied in 78% of the projects they studied, while Hirschman's positive hiding hand, which they termed the *benevolent hiding hand*, applied to only 22% of the projects.

Even if negative effects of overoptimism should be more common than positive effects in infrastructure and other types of projects, there may still be more benefits than costs across all such projects for society at large. With a few projects yielding immense benefits and fewer projects being detrimental, it would not be that bad to have a high number of overoptimistic cost–benefit analyses after all. However, we have yet to see systematic studies on the distribution of benefit outcomes for large projects.

A tendency towards overoptimism may be a result of a supportive and friendly *environment* that does not punish failures too much. Overpessimism, on the other hand, may be a result of a more unfriendly environment. There is a fascinating line of research that shows how humans and animals, for instance, dogs, rats, and starlings, seem to develop more overoptimistic expectancies in better environments [16].

In a study of birds' behaviour, the researchers exposed starlings to both bad and good cage conditions. The bad conditions included unpredictable feeding and cleaning times in a small, boring cage. The good cage conditions included continuous access to water baths, perches made from natural branches, and bark chipping on the floor. The birds first learned that they could receive food pellets if they pressed one lever when they saw a light for two seconds and another lever when the light appeared for 15 seconds. From previous studies, the researchers knew that the birds preferred to receive food immediately, making the two-seconds lever a more positive experience. On some occasions, the light appeared for intermediate intervals, between two and 15 seconds. These were durations for which the birds did not have pre-learned responses. Would the birds believe that the intermediate durations were signals for the pleasant, immediate rewards or the less pleasant, delayed reward? The researchers found that the birds in the good cage conditions tended to interpret the ambiguous light duration as belonging to the most positive outcome and pressed the lever for the immediate food response outcome more often, while those in the more depressive cage conditions interpreted ambiguous light duration more accurately and pressed the 15-second lever when the duration was closer to 15 seconds and the two-second lever when the duration was closer to two seconds. In this context, the less optimistic birds actually received more food due to their more accurate perceptions.

What can we learn from this? Friendly environments and healthy minds may result in overoptimistic predictions, for both birds and people, even when one would benefit from more realistic predictions. If you always see the world through rose-coloured glasses, you can reassure your perhaps somewhat annoyed friends, colleagues, and family that it is more likely a sign of a happy and supportive environment than a diagnostic criterion for a delusional disorder.

Take home message: There are several positive sides of being overoptimistic regarding time usage. Overoptimistic predictions may:

- Compensate for pessimistic beliefs regarding our creativity and problem-solving abilities. If problems happen along the way, we have a good chance of solving them.
- Be essential for innovations.
- Benefit society at large.
- Be a sign of a friendly and supportive environment.

4.3 The Desire to Control Time

Motivation to perform a task efficiently may result in lower time predictions, as well as lower actual time usage. The evidence suggests that the decrease in time predictions due to higher motivation to perform efficiently is frequently *not* matched by the decrease in actual time usage. Consequently, strong motivation to quickly complete work tends to lead to overoptimistic time predictions.

This tendency was documented in a study where participants were divided into two groups. The participants in one group received monetary rewards for being among the fastest performers of an origami (paper-folding) task. Participants in the other group were given the same task but did not receive any monetary rewards. The time predictions of the participants in the first group were, as expected, typically lower than those of the other group. The actual time usage, however, was, on average, about the same for both groups, leading to more overoptimistic time predictions for those who could earn rewards for fast performance [17].

A similar effect may be at play when people are motivated to finish tasks quickly because the tasks are perceived as important [18]. It makes sense that people think they will work harder and more efficiently if tasks are important or if they are rewarded for fast performance. The main mistake seems to be an overestimation of the flexibility of the work and performance. Many types of work and performance are not flexible enough to be completed substantially faster than normal, even when the motivation is strong.

The tendency of higher optimism when motivated to finish fast is more pronounced for people with a desire for control [19]. When motivated to finish fast, those scoring high on the personality trait desire for control predicted lower time usages even for a task that was completely uncontrollable, such as the time it would take to watch a bowl being filled with tap water. Thus, there seems to be a link between overoptimistic time predictions and a general motivation to control things. This is further suggested by results from a study on power and time predictions. One group of people was influenced to think that they were powerful by writing a vivid report of a situation in which they had power over another individual. Another group was influenced to think that they lacked power by writing about a situation in which other people had power over them. All the participants were then asked to predict the time needed to complete a formatting task. Those who were influenced to feel powerful gave more optimistic predictions regarding the time it would take to complete the task. In addition, those with a general feeling of being powerful, based on self-ratings on statements such as 'I can get others to do what I want', were found to give more optimistic time predictions [20].

Take home message: The motivation to do something quickly and the desire for control tend to result in lower time predictions. These two factors may lead to a reduction in the actual time usage through increased efficiency, but this reduction is typically not enough to compensate for the lower time predictions.

4.4   Motivation to Make Accurate Time Usage Predictions

Does greater motivation to produce accurate time predictions lead to higher accuracy? Previously (Sect. 3.7), we gave an example of how rewarding project leaders with high time prediction accuracy led to higher time predictions and a reduction in productivity to make the actual time usages fit the time predictions. Is this what normally happens?

In a study on incentives, some participants were told that they would receive $2 if they managed to predict their time usage to be within one minute of the actual time usage and $4 if they predicted it to be within 30 seconds [21]. Participants in a control group were also asked to predict time usage but received no monetary incentives for accuracy. The participants in the first group, with incentives to provide accurate time predictions, tended to predict too high and less accurate time usages than those in the control group. In this context, the participants did not lower their productivity to make their predictions more accurate, as in the previously described real-world case with project managers, indicating that the effect of higher motivation for time prediction accuracy on work productivity is task and context dependent.

Non-monetary incentives are also candidates for increasing the accuracy of time predictions. Time prediction accuracy was, for example, reported to increase when software developers and managers were made more accountable, that is, when the time prediction accuracy was part of the company's performance review of those in charge of the time predictions [22]. Similar results have been reported by other studies. Note that the higher accuracy may not mainly be a consequence of better time predictions or higher time predictions; it may be, instead, a consequence of a stronger emphasis on adjusting, typically reducing, the work content and quality to fit the time prediction [23].

When overoptimistic time predictions are penalized but accurate time predictions are not necessarily rewarded, we will most likely see a tendency towards more pessimistic, higher time predictions. An example is that waiters who predict customers' waiting times to be seated tend to exaggerate their time predictions to avoid the negative consequences of angry customers [24].

Take home message 1: Rewards for accurate time predictions tend to produce higher but not necessarily more accurate predictions.

Take home message 2: It is risky to reward accurate time predictions or penalize overoptimistic time predictions. Attempts to optimize prediction accuracy may come at the expense of other goals, such as productivity and quality.

4.5 Selection Bias

'We only win contracts when we have been overoptimistic about how much time it takes to complete the work', was the frustrated comment of a software company manager. His company had, for the nth time, won a large contract only to discover that the prediction of time usage, the basis of the company's price offer, was far too low. In situations in which the company had a great amount of relevant experience and was more likely to be realistic about the time usage, it was less likely to be selected due to its higher bid price.

This real-life experience suggests that, even in a world without a tendency towards overoptimistic time predictions, we will still observe more time overruns than underruns. This phenomenon may sound strange but it is a logical consequence of *selection bias* and that we only observe the accuracy of time predictions that lead to action. The projects most likely to be started are those assessed to have the most favourable prospects, typically including overoptimistic views of the required time usage. Such selection bias, when applied to bidding at auctions or offering a price in competition with others, is usually termed the *winner's curse*. The frustrated software company manager may think that the company has had bad luck because it only wins projects when it is being overoptimistic. The client may think that nearly all software companies have overoptimistic time usage predictions, because they nearly always incur time overruns. In reality, both are causing the observed tendency towards overrun: the software company, because it is not compensating for the winner's curse (selection bias) when pricing its projects,[2] and the client, by emphasizing low price as a selection criterion.

To better understand the importance of selection bias in creating time and cost overruns, assume 10 painters offer to paint your house. Each of them predicts the time they will need for the job and they give you a price based on that. The painters vary in how fast they work and none of them knows exactly how much time they will need to complete the job. For the sake of simplicity, assume that it is just as likely that a time prediction is too high as it is too low, that is, unbiased time predictions, and that the painters do not react strategically to your selection strategy. Consider the effects of the following painter selection strategies.

- **Select the best painter**: You do not care about the price and select the painter you think is the best. If everybody did this, there would be no tendency towards overoptimistic time predictions for paint jobs. In most cases, however, it is unreasonable to assume that price is no issue. Completely ignoring price has, for example, the unfortunate side effect that the price of hiring a painter soon goes through the roof.
- **Select the painter with the average price**: The strategy of selecting the average price may seem strange but it has been used as an approach to reduce the problems related to selecting overoptimistic bidders [25]. This strategy may remove the tendency towards overoptimistic time predictions but may also lead to price manipulations in bidding contexts. If a painter collaborates regarding the bid price (colludes) with another painter, they may manipulate the average price and make higher bids more likely to be selected. It might also be difficult to motivate clients to select bids substantially higher than the lowest ones.
- **Select the painter with the lowest price among those assessed to have sufficient competence**: This strategy, which may be the most common, typically means selecting a painter with a lower than average price. This means being more likely to select among those painters with overoptimistic time predictions. You will consequently tend to experience overoptimistic time predictions even if there is no general tendency towards overoptimistic time predictions among the painters.

If we emphasize a low predicted time usage or a corresponding low price when choosing painters, carpenters, software companies, and so forth, we are very likely to experience the world as a place full of overoptimistic time and cost predictions. We may complain about painters who never finish in time or carpenters who provide much lower quality than expected due to overoptimistic time predictions but, in fact, it is very much us and our strategy of selecting the lowest offers that have created this

---

[2]It is not obvious how the person or company making the offer can avoid the winner's curse. Common advice is to add more contingencies (raise the price required for the work in accordance with the level of uncertainty and the number of other bidders) if there is a high risk of only being selected when overoptimistic about the time usage. This raises the question of how much contingency to add and how much the probability of being selected is reduced when raising the bid, especially when not all the providers make the same type of winner's curse–based price adjustments. Sometimes the best option may be to avoid making offers in situations with a high risk of the winner's curse.

world of overoptimistic time predictions. The degree of this overoptimism increases with greater prediction uncertainty, a stronger emphasis on low price when selecting bidders, and higher numbers of predictions from which to select [26].

An underlying problem is that we typically do not know the extent to which a low time prediction is a reflection of higher competence or a consequence of greater overoptimism. Skilled people can do the work in less time and should predict lower than average time usages. Lower time predictions may, on the other hand, also be a consequence of lack of skill in terms of not realizing the extent and complexity of the work. The latter case is called the Dunning–Kruger effect: those who know less know less about what they do not know; in short, they are unskilled and unaware of it [27].

The Dunning–Kruger effect was illustrated in a study of 35 software companies predicting the time usage and cost of the same software project [28]. Seventeen of the companies were allowed to gain more knowledge about the project by participating in a pre-study phase. Those companies made bids, on average, as much as 70% higher than the companies with less knowledge about the required time usage to complete the work. The study also found that the companies with experience from similar projects made bids about 60% higher than those without this experience. If you are a client with a strong focus on low price and a correspondingly lower focus on selecting workers based on their competence, you may consequently experience a tendency towards not only overoptimistic time predictions but also towards selecting less competent workers.

That said, if you exclude potential providers because they gave the lowest time predictions, this may have the unfortunate consequence of you bypassing the most skilled providers. We once asked seven companies to bid for and then complete the same software development project. In this case, the company with the lowest time prediction by far (only 18% of the median time prediction) turned out to be the most competent. That company managed, to our great surprise as clients, to finish on time, with the predicted use of work hours, and with good quality [29]. Not knowing the reason for a very low time prediction, which could be either the presence or absence of high competence, makes the lives of those who select workers difficult.

When we make decisions, such as who to hire for a job or what activity to start, we often try to optimize something, such as value for money, worker competence, or the best quality for a given amount of time usage. A counterintuitive consequence of optimization is that the more we optimize, the more likely we are to be disappointed! Optimizing typically improves the quality of the choice but, since the world is uncertain and our beliefs are inaccurate, the option we select as the best will tend to be less favourable than expected. This effect is referred to as the *optimizer's curse* or *post-decision surprise* [30] and is based on the same statistical phenomenon as the winner's curse.

Given that the best project is typically not as good as it seems, should we then pick the second or third most promising project? Probably not. The best-looking project still tends to be the best. The point is that picking the best alternative makes it more likely that you will be disappointed when comparing your expectations. If you do not like disappointments, be aware that high uncertainty, many options, and a strong focus on optimization lead to projects and options looking better than they actually are.

A solution to the problem of selection bias in the case of time predictions would be everyone increasing their time predictions when expecting to be in a winner's curse situation. Such an increase sometimes develops naturally in mature markets and is then called a *winner's curse effect*, that is, an effect of an awareness of the winner's curse. In situations with more alternatives, greater uncertainty, and stronger competition, the bidding will then be more conservative and, in some contexts, even have the consequence that increased competition actually leads to higher, not lower, time predictions or prices [31].

It is challenging for service or product providers to determine how much to add to the time prediction or cost estimate to avoid the winner's curse. This typically requires information one normally does not have. We found that, for certain typical software development project situations, with five to 10 companies competing for the same project, it may make sense to add about 15% to the time predictions to compensate for the winner's curse [26]. Different situations, however, require different adjustments. In many situations, a better solution than increasing the time prediction might be to emphasize high time prediction accuracy, for example, by providing more and better information and motivate bidders to spend more resources and using better techniques for the time prediction work. When time predictions are accurate, the selection bias effect will be low.

Take home message 1: Even if people's time predictions have no tendency towards overoptimism, the world would still appear to be full of overoptimistic time predictions. This is simply because tasks and options with overoptimistic time predictions are more likely to be selected and lead to action, which is a requirement to be evaluated in terms of the degree of overoptimism. Options with overpessimistic time predictions are less likely to lead to action and will consequently not be evaluated.

Take home message 2: The more we optimize, for example, the more strongly we emphasize low time predictions and low prices when selecting among alternative investments, the more likely the outcome will be worse than predicted. This does not mean that we should avoid optimizing when choosing—only that we should prepare for an outcome less positive than predicted.

4.6   Deception

Norway has a long tradition of winter sports and the city of Lillehammer, with a population of less than 25,000 inhabitants, became the host of the 1994 Winter Olympic games. The original cost prediction of the Olympics was around €100 million, which would result in a financial profit and not cost the Norwegian taxpayers a thing. The International Olympic Committee required the application for the Olympics to have a financial guarantee by the state, which was decided at €180 million. The Norwegian Parliament had no problem providing this guarantee. One reason for this was that the minister responsible was so confident regarding the accuracy of the early cost prediction that he claimed *this guarantee would under no circumstances be effectu-ated*. The parliament gave the financial guarantee without much discussion.[3]

In reality, the Lillehammer Olympics cost close to €1 billion and incurred a financial loss of at least €500 million [32]. When we look at the early cost prediction process, it is apparent that there were strong incentives for underpredicting the costs. The initial prediction of €100 million was provided by the county of Lillehammer. Since Lillehammer would bear little of the cost and receive most of the benefits from the large investments, it had strong incentives to provide low initial cost estimates and to add new cost items after the application was sent to the International Olympic Committee [33]. Similar situations have arisen in many recent infrastructure and construction projects, where parties with a strong interest in starting the projects were involved in the early stages of time usage and cost predictions [34].

Does the very strong underprediction of time usage and cost in the Lillehammer Olympics and other project situations mean that people are *lying* to have projects started and investments accepted? Or is it the case that people actually believe—per-haps because they want to—in their overly optimistic time and cost predictions?

It would be naïve to think that people never deliberately underpredict time usage or costs to have projects, actions, or investments approved [35]. In a study on infras-tructure projects, a transportation planner stated [36]:

> You will often, as a planner, know the real costs. You know that the budget is too low but it is difficult to pass such a message to the counsellors [politicians] and the private actors. They know that high costs reduce the chances of national funding.

Another study, with software professionals, reported that some managers inten-tionally produced too low time predictions to create projects that would look more attractive for top management making the decisions [37].

The strategy of making projects look better than they are by lowering the time or cost prediction is an instance of deception if people give predictions in which they do not believe. It may also count as deception if management simply lowers the predictions given by their project managers or developers without a reasonable argument for lower time usage or costs. A decrease in the time predictions would, however, be the result of good intentions and not deception when based on plausible arguments, such as suggestions related to reducing the content of the delivery or simplifying the solution.[4] So, how much of the overoptimistic predictions are due to deception or lying?

Attempts have been made to quantify the amount of lying in time predictions. In a survey of information technology (IT) professionals, 66% reported having lied in

---

[3]This strong belief in the accuracy of the prediction was amazing, given that all previous Winter and Summer Olympics had cost overruns. The next time Norway made a bid for a Winter Olympics (for the 2022 Olympics), later to be withdrawn, there was much more discussion about the realism of the cost predictions and few believed in the cost predictions, which were likely more realistic than for the Lillehammer Olympics. The media and people in general had, since 1994, learned a great deal about the typical realism of the cost predictions of Olympic Games.

[4]Removing work from a project which already has been time predicted and ask for a new prediction tends to increase the overoptimism of time predictions. See [38].

relation to predictions of cost and time [39]. The category most frequently chosen by the respondent was that they believed—but did not know for sure or could not document—that lying occurred in 50% or more of projects. The perception of the frequency of lying in software project time predictions varied greatly, from very low (0–10%) to very high (90–100%). Another study of IT professionals found that time prediction distortions, which, in this context, are more or less the same as deception or lying, seldom happened [40]. However, instances in which management required too low time predictions, with no argument on how to reduce the time usage, were believed to be common.

The samples of these two studies were not large and we do not know how representative the selected contexts were or what the lies were about. Nevertheless, the studies demonstrated that overoptimistic time and cost predictions are sometimes best described as lies, deceptions, or deliberate distortions of the time predictions. There are researchers claiming that deception is the *most* important reason for overoptimistic time and cost predictions [41]. While people no doubt sometimes deliberately distort predictions to gain approval of projects from their boss, their colleagues, the public, or politicians, the claim that deception is the most important reason is, at least for time predictions, not well documented.

One potential indicator of deception in time and cost predictions is found in the typical increase of predicted costs from the initial stage, where the decision to invest or not is taken, to the project's startup stage, where the project execution is planned and budgeted [42]. A report on 31 large road projects in Norway found that the average cost overrun was 0%, with a worst case overrun of 37%, when compared with the budgets established at the time of project startup. However, when tracking the history of the projects and looking at the *early* cost predictions presented to parliament as a basis for the decision to start the project or not, the predictions were much more overoptimistic [43]. On average, the projects were now 53% more expensive than initially predicted and the worst case was a project with an actual cost 137% higher than the initial prediction.

The obvious reason why it is difficult to document deceptions is that they are not meant to be disclosed or discovered. Another reason is that it is sometimes hard to establish to what degree a too low time or cost prediction is caused by judgement biases, selection biases, bad luck, or deception. A very low but not impossible time prediction may not always be considered a lie. How unlikely should a time prediction be to be perceived or determined as a lie?

When people in charge of the time predictions openly admit that they gave lower time usage predictions than they believed were possible, we can know for sure that deception was involved—but this rarely happens. Thus, the explanation that people frequently lie when giving time predictions must usually compete with other explanations of overoptimistic time predictions.

Take home message: We do not know how often or when deception is the main reason for overoptimistic time predictions. There is, on the other hand, no doubt that deception arises and does so more frequently when the person or organization making the time prediction has a strong incentive to give a low time prediction, for example, to increase the likelihood of being allowed to start their pet projects.

4.7 Who Makes the Most Realistic Time Predictions?

A famous economist once visited a company producing jeans priced as high as $250 [44]. He concluded that there must be a lot of money out there, given the willingness to pay so much for jeans. Partly based on this insight, he predicted that the inflation rate would become unusually high in the near future and he turned out to be amazingly correct. His prediction led to fame as a prediction expert, especially since most of the other experts made more conservative and less accurate inflation rate predictions. But how good a prediction expert was this economist in reality? Was he right for the wrong reasons?

Forecasters, such as the famous economist above, successful at predicting large changes, have, on average, the *least* accurate predictions [45]. This phenomenon may sound counterintuitive but it has a natural explanation. Predicting large changes from historical performance typically means emphasizing specific information and neglecting aggregated information, such as long-term trends or average productivity. The strategy of reacting strongly to one or very few indicators is more likely to lead to spectacular predictions and, hence, fame if the predictions are correct. Such a strategy, on the other hand, is also more likely to lead to incorrect predictions, due to its overreaction to specific information. Returning to our example, the famous economist was among those with the least accurate predictions in the period after his fame as a spectacular forecaster. This suggests that the main reason for his fame was not exceptional prediction skills, but rather luck and a willingness to use specific information (e.g. sales figures for expensive jeans) instead of aggregated information.

There are several domains where luck and bad luck—and not prediction skill—explain most of the variance in the prediction performance. There are even domains, such as stock market investment, where all or nearly all of the variance of forecasters' prediction performance seems to be random.[5] Time prediction performance may not be as bad as that, but there seems to be large element of random variance in who makes the most accurate time predictions.

Even if we cannot expect anyone to consistently predict time usage accurately in contexts with uncertainty, it is meaningful to try to find out more about the characteristics of people who tend to give more accurate time predictions and in what settings they are more accurate. The research on this does not give very clear answers. Nevertheless, some connections, and lack of connections, between personal characteristics and prediction error are worth reporting.

---

[5]We once conducted a study (unpublished) of the correlation between Norwegian mutual funds' performance one year and the following year for the period 2003–2015. The average correlation was as low as 0.025 (0.06% explained variance). See also [46].

Women versus men: We all know it: women are more rational than men. They fight less, care more about other people, and perform better than men in most tasks that require a brain. For example, an analysis of the Programme for International Student Assessment data from 2000 to 2010 shows that girls outperform boys in 70% of the countries, whereas boys outperform girls in only 4% of the countries [47]. Should we perhaps leave the time prediction and planning work to women?

Most time prediction studies, even those where the participants are asked to indicate their gender, omit reporting gender differences. This suggests typically no systematic difference in time prediction skill between men and women, because researchers tend to publish anything they find statistically significant, even if it is not part of their original hypotheses. A few studies, on the other hand, have suggested that men are more—but only a little more—overoptimistic in situations involving incentives for fast performance or when performance can be interpreted as a form of achievement [48, 49]. In total, however, we have not been able to find good documentation of when or why men will be less accurate or more overoptimistic than women in time prediction contexts. Most likely, gender is not a good indicator of time prediction accuracy.

Intelligent versus less intelligent people: How about those who perform better at school or in IQ tests? Are they better at making time predictions than other people? Probably not, according to research [50, 51]. At best, they may be slightly more accurate in predicting time for academic tasks. These are tasks they are better at performing in the first place, so if they happen to be slightly better at predicting time for such tasks, this is not very impressive.

People who believe they are good at planning and predicting: Asking people about how good they think they are at predicting time usage does not appear to be a reliable way of finding people who make accurate predictions. On the contrary, overconfidence in prediction abilities may be associated with overoptimistic time predictions. Despite not being a bulletproof personnel selection method for time prediction tasks, there may be something to self-reports of prediction accuracy. Those who say that they are good at planning and at deciding how long it will take to complete a task actually tend to be *slightly* better than those who do not agree with this characterization [52, 53]. Confidence in the accuracy of a particular time prediction, on the other hand, is not a robust indicator of time prediction accuracy [9].

Conscientious people: People who are generally more careful, diligent, and painstaking in life tend to give themselves more time to complete tasks. This can, in some cases, reduce the risk of too low time predictions but, in other cases, it can increase the risk of too high time predictions [54, 55].

Happy-go-lucky people: People who are better at enjoying the present moment and who do not worry much about the future or about past mistakes tend to predict that boring tasks will be completed relatively early. However, such people actually finish later than those who do not possess such qualities [56]. In other words, they are not the type of people you should trust the most when requiring time predictions.

People trained in time prediction: If we could train people to become better at time prediction, this could reduce problems related to cost and time overruns. When time predictions are required, we would then simply select those who have been trained for such work. How do we train people in time prediction and how effective is the time prediction training?

Training in the sense of learning about biases and the use of proper judgement and decision methods seems to have—but beware of the limited evidence—a positive effect on judgement and decision quality [57]. However, the standard training method of learning through feedback and reflection does not seem to work well for time prediction. As an illustration, a learning process called the Personal Software Process [58] includes a time prediction training program with feedback of actual time usage and analysis of reasons for deviation between predicted and actual time usage. Independent empirical studies analysing this training found no improvement in time prediction accuracy from following this program [59, 60]. Similar results were found in another study on the effect of a feedback and lessons learned training program.[6] Those who followed this training program were instructed to spend time reflecting on what went wrong, what went well, and what could be learned from previous accurate or inaccurate time predictions. The training program did not lead to improvements in time prediction accuracy compared to individuals who underwent no such training program.

Amount of task experience: Generally, more experience in completing a task tends to lead to more accurate time predictions. Research participants without experience in completing the Tower of Hanoi puzzle [62] had, for example, more overoptimistic time predictions than those with some experience [63]. It is, however, not always the case that more experience in completing tasks leads to higher time prediction accuracy. Experience may change the way people think about a task. As people gain experience, their mental representation of the task tends to become more abstract, with information stored in a few larger chunks rather than as many smaller entities that represent details of the task. This has the paradoxical effect that more experience can lead to more overoptimistic time predictions. In a study on predictions of the duration of piano tunes, participants brought their own sheet music and were asked to predict the time it would take to play tunes that were recently learned, well learned, and extremely well learned [64]. The piano players gave 48% too high time predictions for recently learned pieces, 11% too high time predictions for well-learned pieces, and 19% too low time predictions for extremely well learned pieces. This pattern was apparent for both novices with an average of six months of experience and advanced players with an average of 11 years of experience. The results suggest that the piano players 'chunked' together larger parts of the well-learned pieces, whereas they were more conscious about the different parts of the more recently learned tunes.

More overoptimistic time predictions among those with more experience were also found in a study where participants were instructed to fold a paper rabbit (an origami task) [65]. The participants were first asked to produce one (low-experience group), three (medium-experience group), or nine (high-experience group) rabbits.

---

[6]See [61]. Note that the time predictions were found to be more accurate due to increasingly greater knowledge about the tasks to be completed, but this improvement was at the same level as for those not following the time prediction training program.

None of the participants received feedback on their time usage. The participants were then asked to predict how long it would take to make three more rabbits. Participants in the low-experience group tended to predict too high a time usage, whereas those in the medium-experience group and, to an even greater extent, those in the high-experience group predicted too low a time usage.

Before we interpret the results above as evidence of a detrimental effect of experience on time prediction accuracy, we should take a closer look at the studies. The piano and rabbit origami studies showed more underestimation with experience but the *accuracy* of the time predictions actually improved with experience. Although the more experienced participants tended to be more overoptimistic, they also held a more accurate view of their own performance. Furthermore, the participants in the two experiments did not receive any feedback on actual time usage. Perhaps the optimism in the high-experience group could have been reduced with feedback [66].

In professional life, the tasks are usually not as well defined as in the rabbit origami and piano studies. Each new action, for example, does not usually follow the previous one in a predetermined sequence. More complex situations seem to increasingly favour the time predictions of people with more experience. In contrast to the piano and rabbit origami experiments, a study of software professionals found that years of relevant project experience improved the accuracy of time predictions [67]. Other studies in similar contexts have shown that professionals with more relevant experience produce higher and more realistic, time predictions [68]. In particular, more relevant experience seems to be related to better ability in identifying required activities to complete a larger task or project and in assessing their complexity [28]. Ironically, this consequence of more experience is not always an advantage for those making the predictions. The ability to identify more required activities and complexities may be associated with higher time predictions and higher predicted costs. If a client selects someone based on low time predictions or price, they may select those with the least relevant experience, because the providers with the lowest bids may have forgotten to include essential activities in their time predictions.

It is essential to distinguish between the *relevance* of experience, in terms of similarities between the previous and current tasks, and the *amount* of experience, for example, the number of years solving tasks in the same domain. While the relevance of the experience has a clear relation to better time prediction accuracy, the amount of more general, not closely related experience usually leads to very little, if any, improvement [69].

Previous time prediction accuracy: A reasonably good and perhaps the best indicator of how much you can trust a person's time predictions is the person's past time prediction accuracy. In a study of software developers, previous time prediction overoptimism was the best indicator of future time prediction overoptimism [9]. Being the best indicator does not mean, however, that this indicator is very good and the study results suggest a large random element in time prediction accuracy, which should not be surprising given the typical wide and long-tailed distribution of time usage for similar tasks. Nevertheless, even an imperfect indicator is better than no indicator and, of all the indicators discussed in this section, this one seems to be the best, together with the amount of highly relevant experience.

Superforecasters: Tetlock and his research team completed a series of studies on what they referred to as superforecasters [70]. This work does not concern time predictions but is very interesting and impressive and has parallels to the findings cited earlier in this section. Tetlock's research team recruited thousands of highly educated people from various professional- and science-related arenas (alumni networks, science blogs, etc.) for a massive prediction contest. The participants made a range of geopolitical predictions, such as 'will the official euro to U.S. dollar exchange rate exceed 1.40 before December 31, 2014?' After one year, the very best of the participants were selected as superforecasters and allowed to continue the contest in an environment where they could post questions and comments to other superforecasters. The superforecasters turned out to outperform the other contestants by a substantial margin in the second and third years of the tournament, that is, they were not just lucky. Even more surprisingly, they beat the predictions of professional intelligence analysts with access to classified information.

Why did the superforecasters perform better than the other forecasters? The study did not give a definite answer, but what distinguished the superforecasters from the other contestants was the following: they were highly motivated, highly intelligent and knowledgeable, enjoyed solving problems, were open-minded, had a scientific worldview, were thinking probabilistically, were willing to admit errors and change course, and were eager to obtain and share information. The research on superforecasters seems to reflect some of the points made above regarding who makes the best time predictions. For instance, time prediction accuracy was higher among those who were good at prediction in the past, accuracy was higher among highly knowledgeable individuals (i.e. specific task experience). Furthermore, the superforecasters were better at thinking probabilistically and using historical information (the essential ingredients of good predictions pointed out in the Chaps. 3 and 6), and information sharing in groups seemed to contribute to better predictions (see Sect. 7.6).

Take home message 1: Much of what we consider good prediction skills is likely the result of random variation and luck.

Take home message 2: There are only a few reliable indicators of who will give the most accurate time predictions and none of these indicators are very good. You will obtain somewhat better time predictions from people with highly relevant experience and from people who have made accurate time predictions in the past.

References

1. Roy MM (2014) Belief in optimism might be more problematic than actual optimism. Front Psychol 5:624
2. Oxford Dictionaries Optimism. See www.oxforddictionaries.com/definition/english/optimism. Accessed Mar 2017
3. Manger T, Teigen KH (1988) Time horizon in students' predictions of grades. Scand J Educ Res 32:77–91
4. Hamilton BH (2000) An empirical analysis of the returns of self-employment. J Polit Econ 108:604–631
5. Massey C, Simmons JP, Armor DA (2011) Hope over experience: desirability and the persistence of optimism. Psychol Sci 22:274–281
6. Scheier MF, Carver CS (1985) Optimism, coping, and health: assessment and implication simplifications of generalized outcome expectancies. Health Psychol 4:219–247
7. Diener E, Chan MY (2011) Happy people live longer: subjective well-being contributes to health and longevity. Appl Psychol: Health Well-Being 3(1):1–43
8. Windschitl PD, Stuart JO (2015) Optimism biases: types and causes. In: Keren G, Wu G (eds) Wiley Blackwell handbook of judgment and decision making. Wiley, Chichester, pp 431–455
9. Jørgensen M, Faugli B, Gruschke T (2007) Characteristics of software engineers with optimistic predictions. J Syst Softw 80(9):1472–1482
10. Alloy LB, Abramson LY (1979) Judgment of contingency in depressed and nondepressed students: sadder but wiser? J Exp Psychol Gen 108:441–485
11. Moore MT, Fresco DM (2012) Depressive realism: a meta-analytic review. Clin Psychol Rev 32:496–509
12. Taylor SE, Brown JD (1994) Positive illusions and well-being revisited: separating fact from fiction. Psychol Bull 116:21–27
13. McKay RT, Dennett DC (2009) The evolution of misbelief. Behav Brain Sci 32:493–561
14. Wikipedia: The Free Encyclopedia Hiding hand principle. See en.wikipedia.org/wiki/Hiding_hand_principle. Accessed May 2016
15. Flyvbjerg B, Sunstein CR (2016) The principle of the malevolent hiding hand; or, the planning fallacy writ large. Soc Res: Int Q 83(4):979–1004
16. Matheson SM, Asher L, Bateson M (2008) Larger, enriched cages are associated with 'optimistic' response biases in captive European starlings (*Sturnus vulgaris*). Appl Anim Behav Sci 109(2):374–383
17. Byram SJ (1997) Cognitive and motivational factors influencing time prediction. J Exp Psychol: Appl 3(3):216–239
18. Hayes-Roth BB (1980) Estimation of time requirements during planning: interactions between motivation and cognition. Rand Corp., Santa Monica
19. Halkjelsvik T, Rognaldsen MT, Teigen KH (2012) Desire for control and optimistic time predictions. Scand J Psychol 53(6):499–505
20. Weick M, Guinote A (2010) How long will it take? Power biases time predictions. J Exp Soc Psychol 46(4):595–604
21. Buehler R, Griffin D, MacDonald H (1997) The role of motivated reasoning in optimistic time predictions. Pers Soc Psychol Bull 23(3):238–247
22. Lederer AL, Prasad J (1998) A causal model for software cost estimating error. IEEE Trans Softw Eng 24(2):137–148
23. Jørgensen M, Sjøberg DI (2001) Impact of effort estimates on software project work. Inf Softw Technol 43(15):939–948
24. Shepperd JA, Sweeny K, Cherry LC (2007) Influencing audience satisfaction by manipulating expectations. Soc Influence 2(2):98–111
25. Bucciol A, Chillemi O, Palazzi G (2011) Cost overrun and auction format in public works. Discussion paper no. 129. University of Padua
26. Jørgensen M (2013) The influence of selection bias on effort overruns in software development projects. Inf Softw Technol 55(9):1640–1650

27. Kruger J, Dunning D (1999) Unskilled and unaware of it: how difficulties in recognizing one's own incompetence lead to inflated self-assessments. J Pers Soc Psychol 77(6):1121
28. Jørgensen M, Carelius GJ (2004) An empirical study of software project bidding. IEEE Trans Softw Eng 30(12):953–969
29. Jørgensen M (2016) Better selection of software providers through trial sourcing. IEEE Softw 33(5):48–53
30. Smith JE, Winkler RL (2006) The optimizer's curse: skepticism and postdecision surprise in decision analysis. Manag Sci 52(3):311–322
31. Hong H, Shum M (2002) Increasing competition and the winner's curse: evidence from procurement. Rev Econ Stud 69(4):871–898
32. Skartveit K (1996) OL-94 og kostnadsutviklingen: en spillteoretisk analyse av kostnadsutviklingen til OL-94 på Lillehammer. Master's thesis, University of Oslo, Norway
33. Bladet Forskning (1994) OL som beslutningsprosess. www.forskningsradet.no/bladetforskning/Nyheter/OL_som_beslutningsprosess/1250810414587. Accessed May 2017
34. Andersen B, Samset K, Welde M (2016) Low estimates–high stakes: underestimation of costs at the front-end of projects. Int J Managing Proj Bus 9(1):171–193
35. Wachs M (1990) Ethics and advocacy in forecasting for public policy. Bus Prof Ethics J 9(1–2):141–157
36. Flyvbjerg B (2007) Policy and planning for large-infrastructure projects: problems, causes, cures. Environ Plan 34(4):578–597
37. Magazinius A, Börjesson S, Feldt R (2012) Investigating intentional distortions in software cost estimation—an exploratory study. J Syst Softw 85(8):1770–1781
38. Jørgensen M (2006) The effects of the format of software project bidding processes. Int J Proj Manag 24(6):522–528
39. Glass RL, Rost J, Matook MS (2008) Lying on software projects. IEEE Softw 25(6):90–95
40. Magazinius A, Feldt R (2011) Confirming distortional behaviors in software cost estimation practice. In: Proceedings of the 37th EUROMICRO conference on software engineering and advanced applications, IEEE, pp 411–418
41. Flyvbjerg B, Holm MS, Buhl S (2002) Underestimating costs in public works projects: error or lie? J Am Plan Assoc 68(3):279–295
42. Cantarelli CC, Flyvbjerg B, van Wee B, Molin EJ (2010) Lock-in and its influence on the project performance of large-scale transportation infrastructure projects: investigating the way in which lock-in can emerge and affect cost overruns. Environ Plan 37(5):792–807
43. Welde M (2014) Kostnadsutvikling i vegprosjekter underlagt KS2 – fra første offisielle omtale til ferdigstillelse. Arbeidsrapport, Concept. www.ntnu.no/documents/1261860271/1262021752/054_Kostnadsutvikling%20i%20vegprosjekter%2016.10.2014.pdf. Accessed May 2017
44. Denrell J (2013) "Experts" who beat the odds are probably just lucky. Harvard business review, April 2013 Issue. hbr.org/2013/04/experts-who-beat-the-odds-are-probably-just-lucky
45. Denrell J, Fang C (2010) Predicting the next big thing: success as a signal of poor judgment. Manag Sci 56(10):1653–1667
46. Ferreira MA, Keswani A, Miguel AF, Ramos SB (2013) The determinants of mutual fund performance: a cross-country study. Rev Financ 17(2):483–525
47. Stoet G, Geary DC (2015) Sex differences in academic achievement are not related to political, economic, or social equality. Intelligence 48:137–151
48. Henry RA (1994) The effects of choice and incentives on the overestimation of future performance. Organ Behav Hum Decis Process 57(2):210–225
49. Henry RA, Sniezek JA (1993) Situational factors affecting judgments of future performance. Organ Behav Hum Decis Process 54(1):104–132
50. Burt CD, Kemp S (1994) Construction of activity duration and time management potential. Appl Cogn Psychol 8(2):155–168
51. Josephs RA, Hahn ED (1995) Bias and accuracy in estimates of task duration. Organ Behav Hum Decis Process 61(2):202–213

52. Francis-Smythe JA, Robertson IT (1999) On the relationship between time management and time estimation. Br J Psychol 90:333–347
53. Kelly WE (2004) College students' accuracy and perceptions of accuracy in predicting the duration of an academic-related task. Individ Differ Res 2:225–230
54. Kelly WE (2000) Conscientiousness and the prediction of task duration: evidence of the role of personality in time prediction. Doctoral dissertation, ProQuest Information & Learning
55. Kelly WE, Johnson JL, Miller MJ (2003) Conscientiousness and the prediction of task duration. North Am J Psychol 5:443–450
56. Pezzo MV, Litman JA, Pezzo SP (2006) On the distinction between yuppies and hippies: individual differences in prediction biases for planning future tasks. Pers Individ Differ 41:1359–1371
57. Lovallo D, Sibony O (2010) The case for behavioral strategy. McKinsey Q 2(1):30–43
58. Humphrey WS (1996) Introduction to the personal software process. Addison-Wesley, Reading
59. Abrahamsson P, Kautz K (2006) Personal software process: classroom experiences from Finland. In: Kontio J, Conradi R (eds) Lecture notes in computer science: software quality, vol 2349. ECSQ 2002 Springer, Berlin, pp 175–185
60. Prechelt L, Unger B (2001) An experiment measuring the effects of personal software process (PSP) training. IEEE Trans Softw Eng 27:465–472
61. Jørgensen M, Gruschke TM (2009) The impact of lessons-learned sessions on effort estimation and uncertainty assessments. IEEE Trans Softw Eng 35(3):368–383
62. Wikipedia: The Free Encyclopedia Tower of Hanoi. en.wikipedia.org/wiki/Tower_of_Hanoi% 2027.05.2016. Accessed June 2017
63. Thomas KE, Newstead SE, Handley SJ (2003) Exploring the time prediction process: the effects of task experience and complexity on prediction accuracy. Appl Cogn Psychol 17:655–673
64. Boltz MG, Kupperman C, Dunne J (1998) The role of learning in remembered duration. Mem Cogn 26:903–921
65. Roy MM, Christenfeld NJS (2007) Bias in memory predicts bias in estimation of future task duration. Mem Cogn 35:557–564
66. Roy MM, Mitten ST, Christenfeld NJ (2008) Correcting memory improves accuracy of predicted task duration. J Exp Psychol: Appl 14(3):266
67. Morgenshtern O, Raz T, Dvir D (2007) Factors affecting duration and effort estimation errors in software development projects. Inf Softw Technol 49:827–837
68. McDonald J (2005) The impact of project planning team experience on software project cost estimates. Empirical Softw Eng 10:219–234
69. Jørgensen M, Sjøberg DI, Kirkebøen G (2000) The prediction ability of experienced software maintainers. In: Proceedings of the fourth european software maintenance and reengineering conference, 2000, IEEE, pp 93–99
70. Tetlock PE, Gardner D (2016) Superforecasting: the art and science of prediction. Random House, New York

Chapter 5
Time Prediction Biases

To a larger extent than we like to think, our judgements and decisions are affected by irrelevant factors. Fortunately, there are patterns to our irrationality. We are, in a sense, *predictably irrational* [1]. These patterns of irrationality are what we call judgement and decision biases. This chapter describes some of the biases relevant to understanding when and why we make systematic time prediction errors. Better knowledge about the biases and fallacies may help us become better at designing time prediction processes and avoiding situations and information that mislead us.

5.1 The Team Scaling Fallacy

Let us say that you enjoy playing with Lego but not building it, so you decide to hire a team to build a Lego model for you. The team will bill you for the total amount of work, that is, the sum of the time spent on the task of all the workers on the team. If you want to minimize your cost, would you hire a two- or four-person team to complete your Lego construction work?

Usually you will benefit from hiring the smaller team, because the four-person team would spend more time coordinating the work and thus cost you more. This expected decrease in productivity with more people was reflected in the time predictions of the participants of a study of Lego-building teams [2]. Those in the four-person teams predicted, on average, that they would spend a total of 30 minutes on the task, whereas those in the two-person teams predicted that they would spend a total of 23 minutes. The two- and four-person teams both tended to predict too low a time usage, but those in the four-person teams gave the most overoptimistic time predictions. The average actual time usage of the two-person teams was 36 minutes, 55% higher than they had predicted, while the average time usage of the four-person teams was 53 minutes, 75% higher than predicted. Although the participants took coordination costs into account, as reflected in the higher time predictions of the four-person teams, they did not do so sufficiently. This finding, that people tend to neglect the true increase in coordination costs with increasing team size, has been

© The Author(s) 2018
T. Halkjelsvik and M. Jørgensen, *Time Predictions*, Simula SpringerBriefs on Computing 5, https://doi.org/10.1007/978-3-319-74953-2_5

named the *team scaling fallacy*. The team scaling fallacy in the Lego-building study was not limited to the people actually doing the building. When external judges, who were students from another university, were asked to predict the total time usage of the Lego-building teams, the omission of coordination costs was even more severe. These judges tended to predict that the four-person teams would, altogether, have a lower time usage than the two-person teams, resulting in time predictions that would produce, on average, 140% time overrun for the four-person teams but only 45% overrun for the two-person teams. When asked about their time predictions, it appeared that the external judges focused more on the benefits of cooperation, such as synergies, than on the costs of coordinating more people.

The team scaling fallacy also seems to arise in the time usage predictions of larger projects. Studies have found that IT projects with more people have a higher likelihood of cost overrun [3, 4]. Documenting the size of the team scaling fallacy using real-life data is somewhat problematic, since we do not know whether more workers lead to greater coordination costs and cost overrun or whether more workers are allocated to projects that are problematic in the first place. The Lego study, on the other hand, does not suffer from such problems in interpretation and reliably demonstrates the team scaling fallacy in a controlled setting.

Another example of neglecting coordination costs is the common belief that merging organizations will reduce costs and improve productivity. Much of the available research contradicts this belief. Consider a small research institute with about 35 researchers that is merged with a larger research institute of about 150 researchers. According to a study on coordination costs in research units, the predicted number of administrative staff required for the small research unit will grow from the seven originally needed for 35 researchers to 12, for their approximately 20% share of the total number of administrative staff needed for an organization of 35 + 150 = 185 researchers. This finding is based on the following evidence-based relation between administrative and academic staff [5]:

$$Administrative\, staff = 0.07 \times Academic\, staff^{1.3}$$

The important property of the formula is its nonlinearity. A doubling in the number of academic staff does not require merely a doubling of the administrative staff but, rather, a 2.5 ($=2^{1.3}$) times increase. When the number of academic staff is 10 times higher, the administrative staff needs to be as much as 20 ($=10^{1.3}$) times larger.

This formula was developed for academic organizations and there may be organizational growth and mergers that lead to much smaller increases or even a decrease in the need for administration. It is nevertheless a useful reminder of how coordination and administration tend to increase nonlinearly with team and organization size.[1] Good project planners and organizers are well aware of this effect, and are able to take the disproportionally higher costs of administration in larger projects

---

[1]The effect of decreasing productivity with increasing team size has been repeatedly documented. One of the first to do so was the French agricultural engineer Maximilien Ringelmann (1861–1931). Ringelmann also found an increased risk of 'social loafing'—lower motivation to contribute—with increased work unit sizes. Frederick Taylor (the father of scientific management) had previously

into account, but it is not uncommon to neglect or underestimate this increase. As an illustration of how coordination costs can increase more than we would intuitively expect, recall that there was as much as a 50% increase in total time usage when going from a two- to a four-person Lego construction team.

Awareness of the team scaling fallacy is also important when predicting time based on past time usage in other projects or tasks. For example, it is *not* a good idea to use the unadjusted productivity of one project to predict the time usage for another project when their team sizes are very different.

Take home message: A workforce that is twice as large tends to deliver less than twice as much output per time unit due to an increase in the need for coordination. When predicting time usage for projects with many people, one usually needs to include a larger proportion of work on project management and administration and assume lower productivity than in smaller projects.

5.2 Anchoring

The anchoring effect may be said to be the king of human biases. Many biases sometimes arise and sometimes do not and, when they do, they tend to be small. Studies on anchoring, on the other hand, hardly ever fail to show large effects. So, what is anchoring?

The most famous study of the anchoring effect involved a rigged wheel of fortune and asked the question 'What percentage of the members of the United Nations (UN) are African countries?' First, the research participants spun the wheel, which stopped at 10 or 65, depending on how the wheel was rigged, and were asked whether they thought the percentage of African countries in the UN was more than or less than the number on the wheel. Following that question, the participants were asked to predict the proportion of African countries in the UN. The difference in answers between two groups of participants, one with the wheel stopping at 10 and another at 65, was striking: those in the first group gave a median prediction of 25% African countries in the UN, while those in the second group gave a median prediction of 45% [6]. It is hard to imagine that the participants would think that a number on a wheel of fortune, that they believed gave a random number between zero and 100, revealed any information about the actual proportion of African countries in the UN. They were, nevertheless, strongly affected by the number presented to them.

Many anchoring studies in time prediction contexts follow the same procedure [7]. Study participants are first introduced to a task description and asked whether they think the task will take more or less time than a given time usage, which plays the role of an anchoring number. Typically, one group of participants is presented a high time usage anchor and another a low time usage anchor. Subsequently, all the participants are asked to predict the time required to complete the task. This

---

identified similar challenges with group productivity in his work on process improvement in the steel industry.

procedure always[2] produces time predictions that are biased towards the anchoring number. Even anchoring numbers that are completely unrelated to the time prediction task, such as digits from Social Security numbers or phone numbers, may strongly affect people's predictions. More relevant numbers, such as the past time usage of a task, is usually—but not always [8]—more potent as anchors than completely irrelevant ones [9].

The relevance of the anchoring bias outside artificial experimental settings is well documented. We found, for example, that software professionals' time predictions were strongly affected by knowledge about what a customer had communicated as an expectation of time usage, despite knowing that the customer had no competence in predicting the time usage [10]. When the software professionals were asked whether they thought they had been affected by the customer's expectations, that is, the anchoring information, they either denied it or responded that they were affected only a little. This feeling of not being much affected when, in reality, one is being affected a great deal, is part of what makes the anchoring bias so potent and hard to avoid.

What if the customer's expectation represents a totally implausible time usage anchor? In an experiment with software professionals [11], we informed one group of participants that the customer expected a task to take about 800 hours (a very high anchor), another group that the expected time usage was 40 hours (a rather low anchor), and a third group that the customer expected the task to take only four hours (an implausibly low anchor). All participants were instructed to dismiss the anchoring information when predicting. Those in a control group, who received no information about the customer's expectations, gave a median time prediction of 160 hours. Those in the high anchor group (800 hours) gave the highest time predictions, with a median of 300 hours. The rather low anchor group (40 hours) gave a median time prediction of 100 hours. The most striking finding was, however, that those with the implausibly low anchor (four hours) gave even lower time predictions, with a median of 60 hours. This group was even more affected than the group given the somewhat more realistic low anchor. Anchoring studies in other contexts show similar results. Even extreme anchors or suggestions, for instance, that the length of a whale is 900 metres (an unreasonably high anchor) or 0.2 m (an unreasonably low anchor), are at least as effective in influencing people's predictions as more realistic anchors are [12]. Thus, the effect of anchors does not always depend on their realism or on a belief that they reveal relevant information.

Anchoring effects are fairly robust to all kinds of warnings and there is so far no efficient strategy to remove the effect. The following are instructions from two different studies on anchoring:

- The client does not want you to be affected by his cost expectation in your esti-mation work, and wants you to estimate the effort that you most likely will need

---

[2]*Always* is a strong claim, but after conducting numerous such experiments, most of them for educational purposes, we feel fairly confident that this is true. It is especially easy to create large anchoring effects in situations in which there is a substantial element of uncertainty involved in the predictions.

to develop a quality system that satisfies the needs described in the requirement specification [11].

• I admit I have no experience with software projects, but I guess this will take about two months to finish. I may be wrong, of course; we'll wait for your calculations for a better estimate [13].

Although the above warnings cast serious doubt on the relevance of the initial time predictions or expectations of the customers, that is, the time prediction anchors, they did not even come close to removing the influence of anchors.

One does not need numbers to produce anchor-like effects. In one study, the exact same software development task was described as either developing *new functionality*, a description usually applied for larger pieces of work, or as a *minor extension*, a description usually applied for smaller, simpler tasks [11, 14]. Those who received the task described as a minor extension gave much lower time predictions than those predicting the time to develop new functionality.

Evidence on the importance of the anchoring effect includes findings from randomized controlled field experiments. In one such experiment, actual software development companies were paid for giving second-opinion time predictions based on project information [15]. Half of the companies received the project information with different variants of anchoring information included. The anchoring information seemed to have a bit weaker effect than what is typically reported in laboratory-based studies. The strongest effect was found for a low anchor, in the form of a short expected completion time ('the work should be completed in three weeks from the startup date'). In reality, a short development period would lead to more—not less—time usage, because a larger team of people would be required to complete the project on time and more people means higher coordination costs. The companies, on the other hand, gave lower time predictions when the development period was short.

A real-life case of the sometimes devastating effect of anchoring involved a Norwegian public agency that invited software companies a few years ago to bid for a software project. As part of the announcement, the company stated that its initial budget was €25 million. The initial budget was based on a so-called informal dialog with the market. As expected from what we know about the anchoring effect, the time predictions received from the bidders typically represented costs close to €25 million. The actual cost, however, turned out to be around €80 million and the project ran into huge problems, partly due to the vast underestimation of cost and time, and was eventually cancelled.[3]

The anchoring effect is sometimes used to our disadvantage, such as setting a minimum payment requirement on a credit card bill. A study found that, if this minimum amount were removed from the bill, the repayment increased by 70% [17]. A low minimum payment, representing a low anchor, on a credit card bill

---

[3] See [16]. The project was restarted and it ran into new time prediction problems but, in the end, it was able to properly predict the time usage, plan the project, and deliver a good software solution to its users.

makes you pay off less debt, which, in the long run, produces higher costs for you and higher profits for those who presented the low anchor value.

There is no single explanation why anchors affect people's time predictions. One explanation is that an anchor triggers associations [12], for instance, a low anchor makes you think about tasks and solutions that are easy and quick to carry out. Another explanation is that people start out at the anchor value and adjust until they arrive at what they think is a reasonable time prediction. Since the range of reasonable time predictions can be large, the first value that seems reasonable after adjusting from the anchor will be too close to the anchor. In other words, people adjust insufficiently [18]. A third explanation is based on conversational norms. If you ask whether my project will require more or less than 30 work hours, I will assume that you believe 30 hours is a plausible prediction or you would not ask such a question. However, as explained above, even anchors based on random numbers seem to have an impact on judgement. A fourth explanation is that the anchor distorts the perception of the response scale [19]; that is, when larger quantities are anchors, such as 300 work hours, two hours does not appear to be much work but, when exposed to shorter durations, such as 15 minutes, two hours seems like a large amount of time. Which explanation is better seems to depend on the context. It is also reasonable to assume that anchoring can be caused by more than one phenomenon [20].

Take home message 1: Anchoring effects in time prediction contexts are typically strong. The only safe method for avoiding anchoring effects is to avoid being exposed to information that can act as a time prediction anchor.

Take home message 2: Anchors come in many shapes and disguises, such as budgets, time usage expectations, words associated with complex or simple tasks, early deadlines, and even completely irrelevant numbers brought to your attention before predicting time usage.

5.3 Sequence Effects

The sequence effect, as several other biases presented later, may be a close cousin of the anchoring effect. When sequence effects occur, the anchor is disguised as a preceding time prediction. If you first predict that it will take 10 minutes to do the dishes, your time prediction for cleaning the entire house may be two hours. If, on the other hand, you first predict that it will take two days to paint the house, your house cleaning time prediction might be three hours. Although we have not specifically tested the above example, studies suggest that such effects on your house cleaning predictions are likely [21, 22].

We evaluated the sequence effect in the context of software development, with software professionals divided into two groups. One group first predicted the time usage of a large task and then a medium large task. The second group first predicted the time usage of a small and then the same medium large task as the first group. The first group predicted a median time usage of 195 hours for the middle-sized task, whereas the second group gave a median estimate of 95 hours for the same task. In other words, their predictions of the medium task were biased towards their initial prediction of a different task [23].

Sequence effects are quite general and appear in most, perhaps all domains. For instance, when research participants predicted the price of 100 chairs from an Ikea catalogue, the predicted prices depended on not only the chair's actual price but also the predicted price given for the preceding chair [24].

Take home message: Your previous time prediction will typically influence your next time prediction. Predictions are biased towards previous predictions, meaning that predicting the time of a medium task after a small task tends to make the time prediction too low and predicting the time of a medium task after a large task tends to make the time prediction too high.

5.4   Format Effects

Time predictions typically answer questions such as 'How long will it take?', 'How many work hours will this require?', and 'How much time do you need?' The responses to these questions involve judging how much *time* one will need for a given amount of work. However, we could turn the question around and ask how much *work* one can do within a given amount of time. Examples of this alternative request format are 'How much of the work are you able to complete within five work days?', 'How many units can you complete before lunch?', and 'Do I have time to eat breakfast before the meeting starts at 9:00?' That is, instead of giving an amount of work and requesting a prediction for the time usage, one can instead give an amount of time and request a prediction for the amount of work to be completed within the given time frame. The basic finding from studies on such *inverted* time prediction formats is that the more work you have lined up and the less time you have at your disposal, the more overoptimistic your time predictions will be.

One of the first studies of the inverted time prediction format varied the number of errands one could complete (six vs. 12 potential errands) and how much time one had at one's disposal (two hours vs. four hours) [25]. Those who had 12 potential errands believed they could complete more errands within the given time than those who had six potential errands. Furthermore, those who were to predict work to be done within two hours believed they would complete more errands per hour than those with four hours available. Consequently, the participants with the 12 errands and only two hours of time available were the most overoptimistic. They predicted that they would be able to run errands within two hours that, in reality, would take about five hours to complete (150% overrun).

We found a similar effect among students predicting the time to read or walk a certain distance. The students gave more optimistic predictions on how far they could walk and how many pages they could read when given a short time frame. When given five minutes to read from a book, the participants predicted that they would read four pages within this time frame (=0.8 pages per minute) but, if given 30 minutes, they predicted that they would read only 10 pages (=0.3 pages per minute) [26]. In other words, reducing the time frame from 30 minutes to four minutes almost tripled the predicted productivity, but hardly the real productivity.

The same format effect arose for IT professionals predicting the time usage to complete software development work. A group of IT professionals predicted how much of a project they would be able to complete in either 20 or 100 work hours. Those given 20 work hours believed they could complete tasks corresponding to about 20% of the project, while those given 100 work hours believed they could complete 50%. This means that the participants with the 20-hour time frame thought they would be twice as productive as those with the 100-hour time frame (1% vs. 0.5% of the total project work per hour).

The format effect may be one of the more important effects to worry about when predicting time or requesting time predictions. Do not ask how much your colleague can complete in 15 minutes or other short periods; instead, it is usually better to ask how much time is needed for a given amount of work.

There are contexts in which the inverted time prediction format seems to be useful. In so-called agile software development, the team considers how many requirements (called user stories) they have been able to complete in the previous weeks and uses this information to predict the amount of work to be completed next week. This approach seems to lead to fairly accurate predictions of next week's work output. Consequently, it could be that the inverted format is mainly problematic when we lack or ignore historical data on productivity.

Take home message: When the time frame is short and a large amount of work must be done, the inverted request format, 'How much do you think you can do in X hours?', tends to lead to more overoptimistic time predictions.

5.5 The Magnitude Effect

The magnitude effect is the observation that the time usage of larger tasks tends to be underestimated by a greater amount, in both percentage and absolute underestimation, than the time usage of smaller tasks, which may even tend to be overestimated. The effect is easily observed when, for example, comparing the time and cost overrun of multimillion-euro projects with those of smaller projects [4].

Although the larger time and cost overruns for large projects are frequently reported in the media and the association between task size and overrun is extensively documented in research, there are good reasons to believe that the effect is exaggerated and sometimes does not even exist. One reason for an artificially strong association between project size and time overrun is that actual time usage is used both as a measure of task size and as part of the time prediction accuracy measure (coupling of variables). Why this would create an artificial or exaggerated association between project/task size and overrun is a bit difficult to explain, but let us try in an example. Consider the following two situations.

Situation 1: The task size is measured by the actual time usage

Assume that several workers with about the same experience are asked to execute the same task, independently of each other. A reasonable time usage prediction would be the same number of hours for all of them. Let us say that we predict the task will take 100 hours for each worker. Even though their experience levels are very similar and a reasonable predicted time usage for each of them is the same, we cannot expect that their *actual* time usages will be the same. Some will have bad luck, perhaps get distracted to a larger extent than the others, and spend more than 100 hours, while others may be more fortunate and spend less than 100 hours. Since we predicted 100 hours for all of the workers, we underestimated the time for the workers with bad luck and overestimated the time for the lucky workers. If we use actual time usage as our measure of task size, we see that the 'large tasks', defined here as those with an actual time usage greater than 100 hours, were underestimated and the 'small' tasks, defined here as those with an actual time usage under 100 hours, were overestimated. In other words, the use of actual time usage as our task size measure has created an artificial magnitude effect where increased task size, measured as an increased actual effort, is associated with an increased time overrun. On the other hand, we do know that there is no real connection between time overrun and the true task size, since the task is exactly the same for all workers. The connection between task size and overoptimistic predictions is just a result of random variation in the actual time usage, the degree of luck and bad luck, and the fact that we used actual time usage as our measure of task size.

Situation 2: The task size is measured by the predicted time usage

People's time predictions have random components. The randomness of people's judgements may be caused by predictions made earlier that day, by what comes to mind at the moment they make the prediction, individual differences, and so on. This randomness in time prediction, similarly to the randomness in actual time usage, can create an artificial association between task size and time overrun. Assume that several people predict the time they need to complete a task. The task is the same for all of them and requires 100 hours, independent of the person completing it; for example, the task may be to watch eight seasons of the Andy Griffith Show. In this case, people who predict more than 100 hours will overestimate the time usage and those who predict less than 100 hours will underestimate the time usage. If we use the *predicted time* as our measure of task size instead of the actual time as in the previous example, we have a situation in which the 'larger' tasks—which are not truly larger but just have higher time predictions—are overestimated and 'smaller' tasks—those with lower time predictions—are underestimated. As in Situation 1, there is no actual relation between the true task size and the degree of over- or underestimation. The observed association is simply a result of random variation in time predictions and the fact that we used predicted time usage as our measure of task size.

The above two situations illustrate that we should expect greater time overrun for larger tasks when the task size is measured as the actual time usage (or cost) and greater time underrun for larger tasks when the task size is measured as the predicted time usage (or budgeted cost). This was also the case in a comparison of the results from 13 different studies on the magnitude effect [27]; all seven studies that had used *actual* time or *actual* cost usage as the measure of task size found greater underestimation of larger tasks. This finding is in accordance with the common claim that overrun increases with increasing task size. In contrast, the studies that used *predicted* time usage or *budgeted* cost as their measure of task size found little or no underestimation of larger tasks.

So what is the true story about the relation between task size and time overruns? One way of reducing the methodological challenges of studying this relation is through controlled experiments. In controlled experiments, the task size may be set by the experimenter and there is no need to use predicted or actual time as a size measure.[4] One controlled experiment on this topic used the number of sheets of paper in a counting task as the measure of task size [28]. Participants received stacks of paper and predicted how long it would take to count the sheets of paper. An analysis of the time predictions showed that people were more optimistic for larger stacks of paper (larger tasks) than for smaller stacks (smaller tasks).[5] Other controlled experiments with the task size set by the experimenter have shown similar results: larger tasks were more likely to be underestimated than smaller tasks were [26]. In fact, an entire literature shows that people typically underestimate large quantities of any kind (duration, size, luminance, etc.) more than smaller quantities [30].

Consequently, the true magnitude effect, supported by the findings of controlled experiments, is that we should expect greater overestimation, or at least less underestimation, with smaller tasks and greater underestimation, or at least less overestimation, with larger tasks. A natural question is then what constitutes small and large tasks? Not surprisingly, what is perceived as small and large and, consequently, the magnitude effect depends on the context.

An experiment on time perception may serve as a good example of how the context defines whether a task is small or large [31]. In this experiment, people watched a circle on a computer screen for varying amounts of time (between 494 milliseconds and 847 milliseconds) and were asked to reproduce this interval by pressing the spacebar on a computer keyboard. The data showed that the longer intervals were *underestimated*, whereas the shorter intervals were overestimated. The intervals in the middle of the distribution were rather accurately estimated. The next week, the participants repeated the procedure but, now, with a change in the range of the intervals (between 847 and 1200 milliseconds). In the first session, the 847-milliseconds interval was the longest and most underestimated, but in the second session it was the shortest and was consequently overestimated. This rather elaborate experiment

---

[4]The experimental manipulation means that we neutralize the effect of the random variation in the measure of task size; that is, task size is not a random variable but, instead, a variable fixed by the experimenter.

[5]A reanalysis presented in [29].

(each participant was required to produce about 4500 judgements) demonstrates that larger stimuli are underestimated by greater amounts than smaller stimuli are and that the context establishes what is considered large or small. By the way, this result was also thoroughly documented in a study published in 1910, more than 100 years ago [32].

The experiment described above shows how judgements are biased towards the middle of the distribution of a set of durations. Usually, in the context of time predictions, we do not know this distribution and we do not know what kind of information people take into account in their mental representations of typical or middle time usage. It is, for example, possible that the time it usually takes to drive to work influences time usage predictions in other situations, such as predictions of time spent walking to the nearest grocery store from home. The research on the influence of prior time usage experience, distributions, and time usage categories on time predictions is very limited.

Time prediction biases, by definition, describe systematic deviation from reality. Biases should consequently be avoided. When it comes to the magnitude bias, however, it is not obvious that we can or should try to avoid it, especially when the prediction uncertainty is high. Adjusting judgements towards the centre of the distribution of similar tasks will inevitably produce a magnitude bias, where larger tasks are underestimated and smaller tasks are overestimated. In the long run, however, this tendency or strategy actually provides more accurate time predictions. Time predictions are inherently uncertain and the best strategy in the face of this uncertainty is often to be conservative and rely on the middle time usage of similar tasks. The more uncertain you are, the more you should adjust your time predictions towards the middle time usage of previously completed tasks. When high average time prediction accuracy is the goal, there may be no need to correct for the magnitude bias.

What about large projects with major time and cost overruns? Are those overruns the products of magnitude bias? The experimental research on magnitude effects concerns small or extremely small tasks and we do not know how much or whether a magnitude effect plays a role in the time overruns of larger projects. The magnitude effect does, however, seem to be at work when predicting the time usage of software development tasks that are parts of larger projects. Dividing software development tasks into smaller subtasks, for example, has been observed to increase the prediction of the total time usage [33].

Take home message 1: Larger projects have been frequently reported to suffer from greater underestimation than smaller projects (magnitude bias) but, with observational data (as opposed to controlled experiments), this association between task size and prediction bias may be due to statistical artefacts.

Take home message 2: Controlled experiments, avoiding the statistical problems of observational studies, suggest that a magnitude bias actually exists, at least for predictions of relatively small tasks.

Take home message 3: Predicting that the time usage is close to the average of similar tasks will result in a magnitude bias but may also increase the accuracy of the predictions in situations with high uncertainty.

5.6 Length of Task Description

A group of software developers was asked to predict the time they would need to develop a software application. The software application was described as follows:

> The application should take one picture every time 'ENTER' (the Return key) is pressed. New pictures are taken until the person is satisfied and selects one of them. During the picture taking and selection process, the last 20 pictures should be displayed on the screen. The selected picture should be stored on the hard disc as a.jpg file with proper naming. The application should run on a Microsoft Windows XP platform and work with an Apple iSight web cam that features auto focus. This camera comes with a Java interface, and is connected to a Dell Latitude D800 laptop. The laptop is connected to the local area network available at the premises (10 Mbit/s).

Another group of software developers received the following, longer task description:

> The application should take one picture every time 'ENTER' (the Return key) is pressed. New pictures are taken until the person is satisfied and selects one of them. During the picture taking and selection process, the last 20 pictures should be displayed on the screen. The selected picture should be stored on the hard disc as a.jpg file with proper naming. The application should run on a Microsoft Windows XP platform and work with an Apple iSight web cam that features auto focus. This camera comes with a Java interface, and is connected to a Dell Latitude D800 laptop. The laptop is connected to the local area network available at the premises (10 Mbit/s).
>
> The e-dating company sugar-date.com specializes in matching e-daters (people looking for a friend/partner/etc.) based on an extensive personal profile with 70 dimensions. The profile is based on questions that are carefully formulated and selected to establish and enable the matching of the preferences of both young and old. The matching process is performed by a sophisticated algorithm that has been developed by leading researchers in psychology. The matching process results in, for each of the relations to other members of a database of people, a score between 0 and 100. This unique system has received worldwide attention. In fact, many of the features in their matching processes have led other major e-dating companies to change how they do their matching of e-daters. The e-dating system on sugar-date.com is also used for e-dater parties—these are large dating party events, held at up-class restaurants and clubs. At the premises, PCs, digital cameras and printers provide each e-dater with a card showing the photo of the 18 other e-daters present who are their best e-dating matches (highest scores). As members arrive at the party, they are guided to one of many locations inside the premises where they can have their photo taken. The photo is attached to their profile and printed on the cards of those who have them as one of their 18 best matches. Many of the members are concerned that they look good on the photo (naturally), so several shots are often necessary. At present, the photographing process is quite slow, due to the many manual steps involved in taking, picking and storing the photos. The managers of sugar-date.com are as always eager to improve their business processes and are not satisfied with the current photo capturing.

If you read the two task specifications carefully, you will, probably even without any software development competence, see that they have the first part in common and that the text added for the second group does not add any information useful for developing the software. Rationally speaking, the task is the same and the time predictions should be the same for the two groups. The experiment, however, found that the longer text led to substantially higher time predictions. The median time prediction was 66 work hours for the short version and 90 work hours for the longer version [14]. The software developers seemed to have used the length of the description and not just the actual work requirement as an indicator of the time required for the task. Similar effects were found among students, who predicted that they would need much more time (40% more, on average) to read a text printed on 40 double-spaced, single-sided pages than the same text printed on seven single-spaced, double-sided pages [34].

Based on the above two studies, one may gain the impression that it is easy to manipulate time predictions by increasing or decreasing the length of the task description. However, this was not the result from a field experiment with software companies [15]. In this experiment, one group of software companies received a specification on a few pages and another group received the same specification on many more pages. The median time predictions of the two groups were about the same. The effects of increased task description lengths on time predictions are remarkable when they occur, but they may not be very large for important time predictions in real-world contexts made by people experienced in the task.

Take home message: Longer task descriptions tend to increase the time predictions, but the effect may be weak for important real-world time predictions by people with relevant experience.

5.7 The Time Unit Effect

Do you feel that 365 days is longer than one year? Most people seem to feel that way. The likelihood of starting a diet is, for example, higher when the diet program is framed as a one-year plan rather than a 365-day plan [35]. If you find this effect amusing, an even more remarkable and frightening result was reported in a study on judges [36]. Active trial judges were given hypothetical cases and asked to decide what would be the appropriate length of the prison sentences for the offenders. One group of judges was asked to give sentences in months and the other group was asked to give sentences in years. The average length of the sentences, when given in years, was 9.7 years, whereas the average length of the sentences for the same crimes, when given in months, corresponded to 5.5 years (66 months). So, if you happen to commit a crime, you should really hope that the judge gives your sentence in months, or, perhaps even better, in weeks or days, rather than in years.

If we feel that 365 days or 12 months is longer than one year, we should also think that it is possible to complete more work in the same time frame when the prediction uses a time unit of fine granularity, that is, a unit that leads to high numbers. For instance, we should feel that we are able to complete more work in 40 work hours than in five work days of eight work hours each. Being affected not just by the actual magnitude of the work, time, or other quantities but also by the nominal values used to describe the magnitude is called the *numerosity effect* [37].

The numerosity effect is not the only reason we should expect higher time predictions when using, for instance, work weeks rather than work hours. The unit itself may indicate what the person requesting the prediction thinks about the time needed. A person would hardly ask how many months a project will take unless the work is considered substantial. Consequently, the granularity of time units may work as a sort of time prediction anchor. Asking for time usage predictions in person-months makes people think of the task as large, whereas asking for predictions in work hours makes people think the task is smaller. The influence of the unit itself is called the *unitosity effect* [38].

We would expect that both the numerosity and unitosity effects lead to lower time predictions with finer granularity time units, as in predicting time usage in work hours instead of work days or person-months. Is this really the case? Can we affect people's time predictions simply by requesting them in a different time unit?

To test this, we invited 74 software professionals, all experienced in predicting time usage, to participate in an experiment [39]. Half of them predicted the software development time usage in work hours and the other half in workdays. The latter group also indicated how many work hours they usually included in one workday to enable a conversion from workdays to work hours. Two tasks were predicted: For the first, smaller task, those predicting time usage in workdays predicted almost twice the number of work hours as those predicting in work hours (88 vs. 45 work hours). For the second task, the relative difference was smaller (335 work hours when predicted in workdays vs. 224 work hours when predicted in work hours) but still substantial and in the expected direction.

The effect of the time unit seems to be less important when predicting the work to be completed in a given amount of time, as opposed to predicting the time to complete a task. In an unpublished study, we asked students how many pages of their psychology book they could read in either half an hour or 30 minutes. The mean values of the predictions were practically identical (about nine pages). We have also conducted an unpublished study on software development tasks that showed no effect of the units when people were asked how much they thought they would accomplish within a given time frame.

Take home message 1: The selection and use of units in time predictions matters. Coarser-granularity units tend to lead to higher time predictions. In a context where overoptimistic time predictions are typical, it is important to avoid predicting time in finer granularity time units, such as work hours for tasks that require several person-months.

Take home message 2: The choice of time units when predicting the amount of work to be completed in a given time seems to have little or no effect, such as in predicting the amount of work that can be completed in two hours versus 120 minutes.

References

1. Ariely D (2008) Predictably irrational. HarperCollins, New York
2. Staats BR, Milkman KL, Fox CR (2012) The team scaling fallacy: underestimating the declining efficiency of larger teams. Organ Behav Hum Decis Process 118(2):132–142
3. Hill J, Thomas LC, Allen DE (2000) Experts' estimates of task durations in software development projects. Int J Project Manage 18:13–21
4. Sauer C, Gemino A, Reich BH (2007) The impact of size and volatility on IT project performance. Commun ACM 50(11):79–84
5. Jamtveit B, Jettestuen E, Mathiesen J (2009) Scaling properties of European research units. PNAS 106(32):13160–13163
6. Tversky A, Kahneman D (1974) Judgment under uncertainty: heuristics and biases. Science 185(4157):1124–1131
7. König CJ (2005) Anchors distort estimates of expected duration. Psychol Rep 96:253–256
8. Løhre E, Jørgensen M (2016) Numerical anchors and their strong effects on software development effort estimates. J Syst Softw 116:49–56
9. Thomas KE, Handley SJ (2008) Anchoring in time estimation. Acta Physiol (Oxf) 127(1):24–29
10. Jørgensen M, Sjøberg DI (2004) The impact of customer expectation on software development effort estimates. Int J Project Manage 22(4):317–325
11. Jørgensen M, Grimstad S (2008) Avoiding irrelevant and misleading information when estimating development effort. IEEE Softw 25(3):78–83
12. Strack F, Mussweiler T (1997) Explaining the enigmatic anchoring effect: mechanisms of selective accessibility. J Pers Soc Psychol 73(3):437
13. Aranda J, Easterbrook S (2005) Anchoring and adjustment in software estimation. Software Engineering Notes 30:346–355
14. Jørgensen M, Grimstad S (2012) Software development estimation biases: the role of interdependence. IEEE Trans Software Eng 38(3):677–693
15. Jørgensen M, Grimstad S (2011) The impact of irrelevant and misleading information on software development effort estimates: a randomized controlled field experiment. IEEE Trans Software Eng 37(5):695–707
16. Lånekassen (2015) Sluttevaluering av LØFT programmet. www.lanekassen.no/Global/Omorganisasjonen/SluttevalueringL%C3%98FT%20Gartner.pdf. Accessed June 2016
17. Stewart N (2009) The cost of anchoring on credit-card minimum repayments. Psychol Sci 20(1):39–41
18. Epley N, Gilovich T (2006) The anchoring-and-adjustment heuristic: why the adjustments are insufficient. Psychol Sci 17(4):311–318
19. Frederick SW, Mochon D (2012) A scale distortion theory of anchoring. J Exp Psychol Gen 141(1):124–133
20. Epley N (2004) A tale of tuned decks? Anchoring as accessibility and anchoring as adjustment. In: Koehler D, Harvey N (eds) The Blackwell handbook of judgment and decision making Blackwell. Malden, MA, pp 240–256
21. Thomas KE, Handley SJ, Newstead SE (2007) The role of prior task experience in temporal misestimation. Q J Exp Psychol 60(2):230–240
22. Thomas KE, Newstead SE, Handley SJ (2003) Exploring the time prediction process: the effects of task experience and complexity on prediction accuracy. Appl Cogn Psychol 17:655–673
23. Grimstad S, Jørgensen M (2009) Preliminary study of sequence effects in judgment-based software development work-effort estimation. IET Softw 3:435–441
24. Matthews WJ, Stewart N (2009) Psychophysics and the judgment of price: judging complex objects on a non-physical dimension elicits sequential effects like those in perceptual tasks. Judgment Decis Making 4(1):64
25. Hayes-Roth BB (1980) Estimation of time requirements during planning: interactions between motivation and cognition. Rand Corp, Santa Monica, CA

26. Halkjelsvik T, Jørgensen M, Teigen KH (2011) To read two pages, I need 5 minutes, but give me 5 minutes and I will read four: how to change productivity estimates by inverting the question. Appl Cogn Psychol 25(2):314–323
27. Jørgensen M, Halkjelsvik T, Kitchenham B (2012) How does project size affect cost estimation error? Statistical artifacts and methodological challenges. Int J Project Manage 30(7):839–849
28. Roy MM, Christenfeld NJ (2008) Effect of task length on remembered and predicted duration. Psychon Bull Rev 15(1):202–207
29. Halkjelsvik T, Jørgensen M (2012) From origami to software development: a review of studies on judgment-based predictions of performance time. Psychol Bull 138(2):238–271
30. Petzschner FH, Glasauer S, Stephan KE (2015) A Bayesian perspective on magnitude estimation. Trends in Cogn Sci 19(5):285–293
31. Jazayeri M, Shadlen MN (2010) Temporal context calibrates interval timing. Nat Neurosci 13(8):1020–1026
32. Hollingworth HL (1910) The central tendency of judgment. J Philos Psychol Sci Methods 7(17):461–469
33. Connolly T, Dean D (1997) Decomposed versus holistic estimates of effort required for software writing tasks. Manage Sci 43(7):1029–1045
34. Josephs RA, Hahn ED (1995) Bias and accuracy in estimates of task duration. Organ Behav Hum Decis Process 61(2):202–213
35. Ülkümen G, Thomas M (2013) Personal relevance and mental simulation amplify the duration framing effect. J Mark Res 50(2):194–206
36. Rachlinski JJ, Wistrich AJ, Guthrie C (2015) Can judges make reliable numeric judgments: distorted damages and skewed sentences. Indiana Law J 90:695–739
37. Pelham BW, Sumarta TT, Myaskovsky L (1994) The easy path from many to much: the numerosity heuristic. Cogn Psychol 26(2):103–133
38. Monga A, Bagchi R (2012) Years, months, and days versus 1, 12, and 365: the influence of units versus numbers. J Consum Res 39(1):185–198
39. Jørgensen M (2016) Unit effects in software project effort estimation: work-hours gives lower effort estimates than workdays. J Syst Softw 117:274–281

Chapter 6
Uncertainty of Time Predictions

There is a degree of uncertainty in all time predictions. We would not even use the term *predict* if there were no uncertainty in our statements about the usage of time for future tasks. A realistic view of this uncertainty is essential, as illustrated in the following real-life case.

A client was hiring a consultancy company to develop a large and costly IT system. The client suggested a risk-sharing contractual model designed so that the cost of work beyond the predicted time usage (used to calculate the target price) would be split 50–50 between the consulting company and the client. The consulting company, however, was so confident about the accuracy of its time prediction that it suggested an alternative risk sharing model. In its model, which eventually was chosen for the project, the client covered more of the cost if there was a time overrun of less than 30%. The consultancy company would, on the other hand, not get paid at all for work that exceeded the 30% time overrun. Apparently, the consulting company believed that the actual time usage exceeding the predicted time usage by more than 30% was extremely unlikely. What happened? The exact figure was not made public, but the consultancy company suffered a large financial loss that could have been avoided if it had accepted the initial suggestion to split all additional costs 50–50. One might think that this was mainly a negative outcome for the consultancy company. After all, the client did not have to pay anything for the additional work. However, it is very difficult to collaborate with contractors who do not get paid for work done. The consequence was a decrease in quality and endless discussions about whether a feature of the software was specified in the contract or should be considered a change order, leading to extra payment. In such cases, the client often ends up paying much of the overrun, receives a product of low quality and low usefulness, and spends costly time in discussions and perhaps even in court to settle disagreements related to payments—all of this due to underestimating the uncertainty of time predictions.

It will probably not come as a great surprise that people generally trust the accuracy of their time predictions to a greater extent than they should; that is, people tend to be overconfident more often than underconfident regarding the uncertainty of their time predictions [1]. This tendency was illustrated in a study in which students were given a software programming assignment [2]. Before completing the assignment,

© The Author(s) 2018
T. Halkjelsvik and M. Jørgensen, *Time Predictions*, Simula SpringerBriefs on Computing 5, https://doi.org/10.1007/978-3-319-74953-2_6

they were instructed to predict the upper limit (maximum) of time usage, a value they were instructed to be 99% sure not to exceed, and the lower limit (minimum), a value corresponding to the amount of time they were 99% sure of surpassing. This minimum–maximum interval is a 98% prediction interval, that is, an interval that should be 98% likely to include the actual time usage. If the students' confidence levels were realistic, one should expect the actual time usage to be outside the intervals for only 2% of the students. After completing the programming task, however, as many as 43% of the students failed to include the actual time usage in their prediction intervals.

Predicting in groups may reduce but does not remove overconfidence. We once asked software professionals, first individually and then in teams, to predict the time usage and provide a 90% prediction interval for a software development project [3]. The prediction intervals given individually were the most overconfident, with only 10% of the actual time usages inside the interval (the intervals should have covered as much as 90%). The team discussion-based prediction intervals were better, including 40% of the actual time usage but still indicating overconfidence. It appeared as team members with conservative time predictions and wider individual prediction intervals had a greater influence on the teams' predictions than the most optimistic and overconfident members did.[1] There is, of course, no guarantee that this will happen in other contexts. Group work may sometimes increase willingness to take risks, as well as probably the overconfidence in time predictions.

Take home message: Expect people, even when working in groups, to be overconfident in the accuracy of their time predictions (i.e., they give too narrow time prediction intervals).

6.1 Why Are We Overconfident?

Why are people overconfident in the accuracy of their time predictions? One explanation is that most people have no way of knowing whether they are 50%, 90%, or 99% confident. We are simply not equipped with good skills, or intuition, in understanding and assessing confidence levels expressed as probabilities.[2]

A demonstration of our limited ability in assessing confidence levels as probabilities is reported in a study where one group of participants was instructed to give

---

[1] Note that whether the actual time usage of a single project is inside or outside a prediction interval is not necessarily a good indicator of an individual's ability to produce realistic intervals. A very high actual project time usage far outside the boundaries of the prediction intervals may, for example, be a consequence of extremely bad luck with the project, that is, a rare situation not meant to be included by the prediction interval.

[2] It is astonishing that so many prediction models, time prediction practices, and project management textbooks are based on the assumption that people are equipped with good judgment on, for example, the minimum and maximum time usages connected with 98 or 90% confidence. This is an unfortunate example of the lack of transfer of research results from the domain of psychology to the domain of engineering and project management.

99% prediction intervals, a second group 90% prediction intervals, a third group 75% prediction intervals, and a fourth group 50% prediction intervals. We would expect that the groups with higher confidence levels also gave wider intervals. This was not the case. All groups gave, on average, about the same time prediction intervals. Other studies have shown similar results. People seem to provide what they consider to be a reasonable low time prediction (the minimum value) and a reasonable high time prediction (the maximum value) more or less irrespective of the confidence level requested [4].

Given the above results, in many contexts, it may be more correct to talk about the *ignorance* of confidence levels in time predictions rather than *overconfidence* [5]. If ignorance of confidence levels is common, we will find that the higher the confidence level you ask for, the more overconfident people will appear to be. For typical software development work, for example, a possible rule of thumb based on various published and unpublished studies is that people's perceptions of minimum and maximum time usage frequently correspond to a hit rate (proportion of actual values included in the predicted minimum–maximum interval) of 50–70% [6]. This means that most people will be overconfident when asked to give a 90% confidence interval, but not when asked for a 50% confidence interval.[3]

Another factor contributing to too narrow, apparently overconfident time prediction intervals is the wish to provide useful information and to be seen as competent (see also our discussion on this topic in Sect. 3.1). A software professional we once interviewed reported that '[wide prediction intervals] will be interpreted as a total lack of competence and has no informative value to the project manager. I'd rather have fewer actual values inside the minimum–maximum interval than providing meaningless, wide effort prediction intervals'. This desire to provide informative intervals seems to be reinforced by managers. In one study, software managers received information about the prediction intervals of two software developers. One of the developers was described as giving wide 90% confidence time prediction intervals and attaining a hit rate of 80%. The other developer gave more narrow 90% prediction intervals of time usage and attained a hit rate of only 60%. Despite the higher degree of realism of the wide interval, most managers preferred the narrow interval and believed that the developer who provided this was more skilled and had greater knowledge of the task. Most managers even believed that the developer with the narrower interval had more knowledge about the task's uncertainty [3]. Furthermore, a study on environmental change predictions suggested that people can perceive narrow confidence interval as signals of *high confidence* (e.g. 90% sure), whereas, in reality, narrow intervals are less likely to include the actual outcome than wide intervals are and should be associated with lower confidence [7].

Take home message 1: Overconfidence in the accuracy of time predictions is often more correctly described as ignorance of confidence levels expressed as probabilities. When unaided by historical data, people tend to give the same minimum and

---

[3]Be aware that the given rule of thumb of a 50–70% hit rate does not apply to all sorts of work. Different contexts will have different hit rates.

maximum time usage values for widely different confidence levels, for example, little difference between 90 and 50% prediction intervals.

Take home message 2: Overconfidence may also be caused by a desire to give informative time prediction intervals and to appear competent.

6.2   What Can We Do to Avoid Overconfidence?

Ignorance of confidence levels, the wish to be informative, and the desire to be perceived as competent may, as claimed in the previous section, explain to some extent the typical overconfidence in time prediction accuracy in high-uncertainty situations. The more important question is whether we can do something about it. While it may be hard to avoid overconfidence altogether, there are methods that seem to improve the realism of time prediction intervals.

6.2.1   The Use of Alternative Interval Prediction Formats

Instead of asking for a minimum–maximum time interval corresponding to 90% confidence, we could turn the question around. We can ask for the level of confidence for a given minimum–maximum time usage interval. If you think 100 work hours is a reasonable time prediction for a certain job, then you could use the time usage corresponding to, say, 50–200% of this prediction (in this case the interval between 50 and 200 work hours) and ask for the probability of the actual time usage falling between 50 and 200% of the predicted time. Studies report a remarkable reduction in overconfidence when using this alternative request format for *wide* time usage intervals [6]. When, on the other hand, the time prediction intervals were *narrow*, this request format did not increase realism [8]. For example, software developers believed that it was at least 60% probable that the actual use of time would be within ±10% of the predicted use of time. In reality, only 15%- and not 60%—of the projects fell within the ±10% prediction interval.

A potential advantage of the alternative format is that it eases the use of historical data. In situations with tasks of varied size and complexity, it is difficult to use historical data on time usage to calculate a 90% prediction interval for a new task. It is easier to use the historical data from tasks of various sizes and degrees of complexity to develop a distribution for the time prediction error. The latter can, together with the alternative interval prediction method, be used to find prediction intervals and pX predictions. This method is illustrated below.

Think about one type of work you often do. How often have you ended up spending more than twice (200%) the predicted time on this type of work? Say that this happens about 5% of the time. This means that it does *not* happen about 95% of the time. In other words, given that history is a good predictor of future prediction errors, you can be 95% confident that you will not exceed twice the work effort of your predicted time usage. This value is then your p95 prediction value. Use the same reasoning to add a lower bound. Look back on previous tasks and assess how often you spent less than 80% of the predicted time (20% underrun) on the task. If you spent less than 80% of your predicted time usage about 5% of the time, your p5 prediction corresponds to 80% of your prediction. By using these two values, the p5 and p95 predictions, as the interval limits, we obtain a (95–5)% = 90% time prediction interval. Given relevant historical data, the actual time usage will be 90% likely to be between 80% (p5) and 200% (p95) of the predicted time. If the predicted time is 100 work hours, the 90% prediction interval is 80–200 work hours.

If you are a manager and ask your employees to use the technique above when predicting work hours, you might end up with a p25 prediction here and a p90 prediction there. If what you really want is, for example, the p50 prediction (which you want to use as your planned time usage) and the p85 prediction (which you want to use as your budgeted time usage), what should you do?

The distribution of potential time usages can be derived from any two pX predictions, given a few assumptions about the underlying distribution of outcomes [9]. As discussed in Sect. 3.4, the distribution of time usage is typically right-skewed with a long tail. We find that a lognormal distribution fits this characteristic well.[4] Based on the assumption of lognormal time usage distributions we have developed a simple tool that helps you derive prediction intervals and any pX prediction based on a time prediction (your best guess of a task's time usage) and two pX values based on past prediction accuracy (i.e. the amounts of overrun and underrun you typically experience with similar tasks).[5]

Example[6]: Assume that you receive a new task and predict it will take about 10 hours. You think back on similar tasks and recognize that, in two out of 10 similar cases, you spent 90% or less of the predicted time (an underrun of 10% or more) and, in eight out of the 10 cases, you spent 150% or less of the predicted time (an overrun of 50% or less). Two pX values associated with your time prediction are easily calculated from this information (see Table 6.1).

The above two pX values can be used to calculate the probability distribution of time usage. This distribution can be displayed as a *density* distribution, as in Fig. 6.1, or as a *cumulative* probability distribution, as in Fig. 6.2. In Fig. 6.1, we see that the most likely time usage is 10.6 hours, that is, a little bit more than the predicted time usage. The model does not care what you think your initial point estimate represents, for instance, whether it is meant to be the most likely, mean, or median time usage or something else. The only thing that matters is that you are reasonably consistent in what you mean with a time prediction and how you measure your prediction error. This means that, even if you think you provided a prediction of the most likely time,

---

[4]There may, however, be a few cases in which we need distributions that can accommodate thicker tails (more 'black swans') than can be represented with a lognormal distribution. See [10].

[5]See www.simula.no/~magnej/Time_predictions_book.

[6]This example is included in the aforementioned tool (the Excel spreadsheet).

Table 6.1 Find two pX predictions based on past time prediction accuracy

Observation	Corresponding pX	pX value when the prediction is 10 hours
In 2 out of 10 times, we spent 90% or less of the predicted time usage (10% or more underrun)	p20	90% of the predicted time usage (0.9 × 10 hours = 9 hours)
In 8 out 10 times, we spent 150% or less of the predicted time usage (50% or less overrun)	p80	150% of the predicted time usage (1.5 × 10 hours = 15 hours)

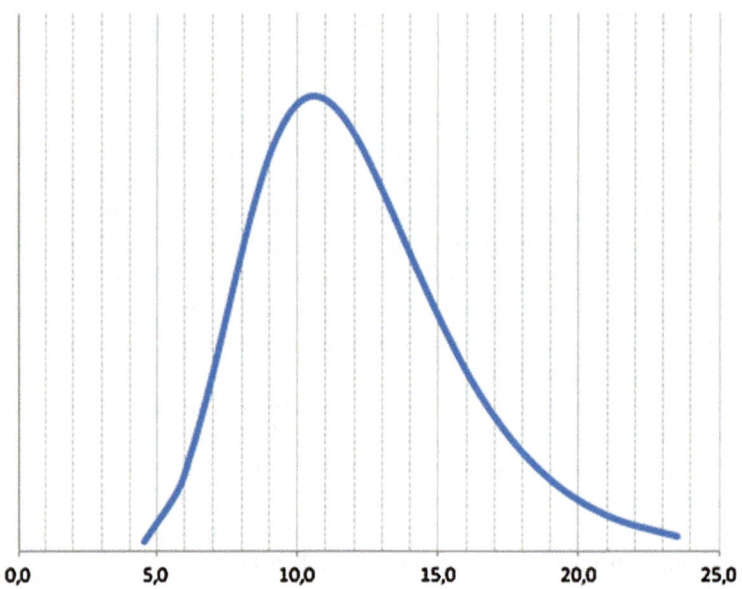

Fig. 6.1 Probability distribution (density) of time usage based on a p20 value of nine hours and a p80 value of 15 hours

the model may give you a different (hopefully better) point estimate of the most likely time based on your input of historical data.

Based on the time prediction and the two pX values from Table 6.1, we can find any pX prediction in the cumulative distribution (Fig. 6.2). The p5 and p95 predictions, for example, can be found to be seven hours and 19 hours, respectively, implying that the 90% confidence interval should be seven to 19 hours. As can also be seen in Fig. 6.2, the two pX predictions we gave as input, the p20 and p80 predictions, still have the values of nine and 15 hours.

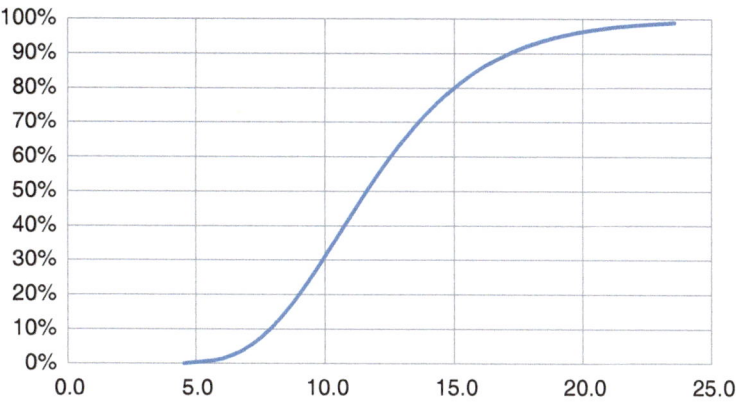

Fig. 6.2 Cumulative (pX) distribution of time usage based on a p20 value of nine hours and a p80 value of 15 hours

Assuming that the input of historical prediction error (or one's judgement of it) is relevant for the task to be predicted and not far off from the actual prediction errors, you can obtain a great deal of other useful information from such a probability distribution. Figure 6.2 suggests, for example, that the task is only about 30% likely to be finished after 10 work hours and 50% likely that it will take 11.6 work hours or less and that you can be pretty sure (around 96%) that the task will be finished within 20 hours.

The prediction intervals and the pX predictions obtained by the method explained here have their limitations. The method is dependent on correctly remembered or correctly recorded time prediction errors of a larger set of previously completed tasks, and it relies on the assumption that the task to be predicted is similar in prediction complexity to the previous tasks. Still, we think that the method will be better at providing realistic time prediction uncertainty information than typical, unaided predictions of minimum–maximum time usage for given confidence levels.

Take home message: We propose a method (with an associated tool) for assessing time prediction uncertainty. The method is based on an alternative way of asking for confidence intervals (that does not require a predefined confidence level) and requests historical information about previous time prediction accuracy. Based on this input, the tool can derive a full distribution of potential outcomes.

6.2.2   Learning from Accuracy Feedback

Repeated feedback about the accuracy of time prediction tasks may increase realism and decrease the level of overconfidence of time prediction intervals. In one study, software professionals predicted the most likely time usage and provided the 90%

time prediction intervals of 30 tasks [11]. The tasks had previously been completed by other developers, so we were able to give the participants information regarding actual time usage after they predicted each task. On average, the 90% confidence intervals given by the participants included only 64% of the actual values for the first 10 tasks, 70% for the next 10 tasks, and 81% for the last 10 tasks. In other words, the realism improved. But even after 20 tasks with accuracy feedback, and even when the participants were not personally involved in the task execution, there was still a bias towards too narrow confidence intervals.

There may be less improvement from feedback when one is trying to learn in a context with greater personal involvement. This was demonstrated in a study of software developers sequentially predicting the time usage, assessing the time prediction uncertainty, and completing five software development tasks [12]. The developers' uncertainty assessments involved a judgement of the probabilities that the actual time usage would fall within 90–110%, 60–150%, and 50–200% of their predicted time usage. Another group, also software developers, received data on the predicted and actual time usages for the first three tasks for one of the developers and then provided uncertainty assessments for the remaining two tasks by the same developer. These developers did not themselves complete any work and were, consequently, less personally involved. The first group, who performed the work, were strongly overconfident, whereas those not involved in the task execution gave more realistic (actually, highly accurate) confidence levels.

Several other studies document that, even after many cycles of predicting time usage, assessing time usage uncertainty, completing tasks, and receiving feedback about actual time usage, people remain overconfident [13]. The lack of learning from experience is especially evident when people are instructed to give high confidence intervals, such as 98% confidence intervals.

Take home message: People tend to remain overconfident in the accuracy of their time predictions even after extensive accuracy feedback, especially when they are personally involved in the task execution.

References

1. Jørgensen M, Gruschke TM (2009) The impact of lessons-learned sessions on effort estimation and uncertainty assessments. IEEE Trans Software Eng 35(3):368–383
2. Connolly T, Dean D (1997) Decomposed versus holistic estimates of effort required for software writing tasks. Manage Sci 43(7):1029–1045
3. Jørgensen M, Teigen KH, Moløkken-Østvold K (2004) Better sure than safe? Over-confidence in judgment based software development effort prediction intervals. J Syst Softw 70(1):79–93
4. Teigen KH, Jørgensen M (2005) When 90% confidence intervals are 50% certain: on the credibility of credible intervals. Appl Cogn Psychol 19(4):455–475
5. Jørgensen M (2014) The ignorance of confidence levels in minimum–maximum software development effort intervals. Lect Notes on Softw Eng 2(4):327–340
6. Jørgensen M (2004) Realism in assessment of effort estimation uncertainty: it matters how you ask. IEEE Trans Softw Eng 30(4):209–217

7. Løhre E, Teigen KH (2017) Probabilities associated with precise and vague forecasts. J Behav Decis Making. Advance online publication. https://doi.org/10.1002/bdm.2021
8. Jørgensen M, Faugli B, Gruschke T (2007) Characteristics of software engineers with optimistic predictions. J Syst Softw 80(9):1472–1482
9. Cook JD (2010) Determining distribution parameters from quantiles. www.johndcook.com/quantiles_parameters.pdf. Accessed May 2017
10. Budzier A (2014) Theorizing outliers: explaining variation in IT project performance. Doctoral dissertation, University of Oxford
11. Jørgensen M, Teigen KH (2002) Uncertainty intervals versus interval uncertainty: an alternative method for eliciting effort prediction intervals in software development projects. In: International Conference on Project Management (ProMAC). Singapore, pp 343–352
12. Gruschke TM, Jørgensen M (2008) The role of outcome feedback in improving the uncertainty assessment of software development effort estimates. ACM Trans Softw Eng Methodol 17(4):1–35
13. Gruschke T, Jørgensen M (2005) Assessing uncertainty of software development effort estimates: the learning from outcome feedback. In: Software metrics, 2005. 11th IEEE international symposium. IEEE, p 4

Chapter 7
Time Prediction Methods and Principles

7.1 Unpacking and Decomposition

The prominent approach for reducing a problem's complexity is to decompose it into less complex subproblems, solve each of these, and then aggregate the subsolutions into an overall solution. In time prediction contexts, this approach is typically the basis of what has been referred to as the bottom-up method, the activity-based method, or predictions based on a work breakdown structure. Generally, across a range of domains, decomposition has been found to improve judgement quality and increase prediction accuracy [1]. In the domain of time predictions, however, there are also situations in which decomposition leads to overoptimistic and less accurate judgements [2].

The time prediction literature has examined two types of decomposition strategies: *unpacking*, which consists of merely listing or thinking about the subcomponents of a task before predicting the time usage as a whole, and *decomposition*, which consists of unpacking, predicting the time usage for each unpacked component, and then aggregating the time predictions into a prediction of the total time usage.

Unpacking: Unpacking tend to give higher time predictions. For example, if you ask people to list all the persons for whom they must buy Christmas presents, they will tend to predict that they need more time to complete their Christmas shopping compared to those who did not generate such a list. Unpacking strategies may be based either on the self-generation of components, as in the example above, or on reminding the participants of possible subcomponents, for example, by using a checklist for activities to be included. Checklists, or reminders, are usually very effective and easy to implement and may improve the accuracy of time predictions, particularly in situations in which there is a tendency towards overoptimistic time predictions [3]. In one study illustrating how unpacking tends to increase time predictions, participants were instructed to format a document to match a printed, edited version of the same document. When asked to predict how long it would take to format the document without any reminders of the work's components, the participants predicted, on average, eight and a half minutes. When asked to predict how long it

© The Author(s) 2018
T. Halkjelsvik and M. Jørgensen, *Time Predictions*, Simula SpringerBriefs on Computing 5, https://doi.org/10.1007/978-3-319-74953-2_7

would take with reminders of the work's components, such as including italics and special characters (ə, ŏ, î), the participants predicted, on average, about 13 minutes [4].

In many cases, the increase in time predictions from unpacking a task contributes to greater realism [5]. Projects that used checklists when predicting time were, for example, more accurate and less overoptimistic (with predictions, on average, 10% too low) than projects that did not (with predictions, on average, 38% too low) [3]. Although unpacking may generally contribute to more accurate and less overoptimistic time predictions, this may not always be the case. Pointing out obvious components of a task, small and simple components, or components that are part of the last steps of a task may not lead to more accurate time predictions [4].

There are also other possible negative effects of unpacking in time prediction contexts. Attempts to identify when, where, and how to complete a task that involves concrete, specific plans of the steps involved may sometimes increase the level of overoptimism. This has particularly been observed in predictions of *when* a task will be completed (completion date) [6]. A step-by-step unpacking of a task may omit important components and focusing on the steps involved may make people think that the task will be performed exactly as imagined, without delays or interruptions, which, in turn, may lead to an illusion of control and overly optimistic time predictions.

Decomposition: Decomposition-based time predictions are based on dividing work into additive or multiplicative components, followed by predictions of the time required for each component, and, finally, aggregating the individual time predictions. Prediction of a project's total time usage may, for example, consist of time predictions of the development of part A (100 hours), part B (400 hours), part C (50 hours), and part D (50 hours), in addition to administrative activities (20% of the non-administrative work), which, in total, yields a time prediction for the project of $100 + 400 + 50 + 50 + 0.2 \times (100 + 400 + 50 + 50) = 720$ hours.[1]

The predicted time usage of smaller tasks is more likely to be overestimated, or at least less underestimated, than that of larger tasks. Since decomposition means predicting the time usage of smaller tasks, we should expect a higher sum of time predictions compared to non-decomposed predictions of the total work. If decomposition means higher time predictions, it means less bias towards too low time predictions for work that tends to be underestimated and stronger bias towards too high time predictions for tasks that tend to be overestimated. This effect was demonstrated in the following two experiments [7].

In the first experiment, two groups of research participants predicted the time of six small office tasks (e.g. delivering letters, making phone calls, and proofreading). One group predicted the total time of the first three tasks and then made separate time predictions for each of the last three tasks. The other group predicted the time of the same six tasks, but with a total time prediction for the last three tasks and separate

---

[1]Note that we are allowed to add the time predictions of the components only when they are the expected (*mean*) time usage of each component. Addition of the most likely time usage values yields time predictions that are too low. See Sect. 3.5 for more details on this.

time predictions for each of the first three tasks. The resulting time predictions were, as expected, higher when predicting the tasks separately (decomposed) than as a whole. In the office task situation studied, the general tendency was towards too high time predictions. This led to a stronger bias towards too high time predictions for the decomposed time predictions. The decomposed predictions were, on average, 9 and 10% too high, whereas the predictions of the tasks as a whole were only 2 and 5% too high.

The time predictions of the second experiment, which also included an office task and two groups of participants, had a general tendency towards being too low. As in the first experiment, the decomposed time predictions were higher but now led to more accurate time predictions. The decomposed predictions were, on average, 0 and 8% too low, whereas the predictions of the tasks as a whole were, on average, 13 and 26% too low.

Other studies have demonstrated that it is not always easy to know when decomposed time predictions will be more accurate. A study on software development, for example, found that decomposed time predictions of software development tasks were, on average, higher but also less accurate than time predictions of the tasks as a whole [8].

Accurate decomposition-based time predictions depend on the successful identification and aggregation of *all* the relevant components or, if that is not possible, the inclusion of sufficient time in the prediction of the total time usage to account for unknown components and unexpected events. Furthermore, aggregation of decomposed predictions requires the prediction of mean values (see Sect. 3.5), and potential dependencies between activities needs to be taken into account. These challenges are not so much an issue for non-decomposed time predictions, such as analogy-based ones. More on that topic in the next section.

Take home message 1: The use of checklists or reminders of work components typically have a positive effect on time prediction accuracy.

Take home message 2: The more you unpack or decompose the problem, the higher the time prediction will be, unless you forget components. Higher time predictions mean lower time prediction accuracy in situations in which tasks tend to be overestimated and higher accuracy for tasks that tend to be underestimated.

Take home message 3: Accurate decomposed time predictions require the successful identification of all components. If that is not possible, sufficient time should be added to account for unknown components and unexpected events.

7.2 Analogies

Judgement-based time predictions are likely to involve some type of recall of time spent on similar tasks or projects in the past, in other words, predictions depend on the use of analogies. For example, when we mentally simulate the completion of a task, visualizing step by step what to do, we somehow have to rely on experience from previous similar tasks to know whether it will take 30 seconds, two minutes, or one hour to perform one of the steps. In this sense, all types of judgement-based time predictions are based on analogies. There is, however, an important difference between the intuition-based (unconscious) use of analogies and their explicit (conscious) use. This section is about the explicit use of analogies.

Analogy-based time predictions sometimes result in improved prediction accuracy. For instance, students completing a computer assignment gave less overoptimistic completion time predictions (delivery date predictions) when they collected and used the time spent on similar previously completed tasks to predict the time on the new task [9]. One benefit of the use of close analogies instead of decomposition is that a realistic number of unknown components and unexpected events, which in a decomposition-based time prediction would have to be properly identified, is often an inherent part of the analogy's time usage. This means that unknown components and unexpected events are incorporated into the analogy-based prediction.

Analogy-based methods, however, have other challenges that must be addressed to achieve accurate time predictions. In particular, it is essential to understand the work we try to predict sufficiently well to find close analogies. If we only have a vague and incomplete understanding of the new task, we will tend to recall less relevant and even irrelevant analogies. The less we know about what we want to predict, the more the work looks like the first analogy that comes to mind, regardless of the true similarity between the current and the previous work.[2]

When the analogies identified are not very close to what we want to predict or when the uncertainty is high, it is usually better to rely on several analogies instead of only one. Unless there are very good reasons for weighting one analogy more than others, a simple average (or preferably the median or trimmed mean) of these analogies is likely to give as accurate time predictions as more sophisticated combination strategies [11]. More on combinations of time predictions in Sect. 7.6.

One or more of the analogies identified may be unusual in one way or another. A task identified as a close analogy may, for example, have been solved with unusually low or high productivity. In such cases, it may make sense to adjust the simple average of the analogies towards the time usage of the average productivity of a broader range of similar tasks [12]. We explain this approach in the example below.

Let us say you want to go hiking to the top of a 1200-metre-high mountain and the distance is about 15 kilometres. You remember that you spent about five hours on your trip to reach the top of a mountain of approximately similar height last year and that the distance was about 14 kilometres (almost the same). Using this hike as your analogy yields a prediction of about five hours for the hike. However, you also know that your typical mountain hiking speed is about five kilometres per hour, which would yield a prediction of three hours for the hike. In other words, it seems you were much slower than usual on the hike you want to use as your analogy. Which prediction should you trust? The one based on the closest analogy or the one based

---

[2]This is an implication of the feature matching theory, when applied to comparisons of task. See [10].

on the average of several not-so-close analogies? A simple rule of thumb for this and similar situations is to use a 50–50 weighting of the closest analogy and the average speed. The new time prediction, which is a hybrid of the analogy- and average-based time predictions, is then (5 hours + 3 hours)/2 = 4 hours.

Generally, when there is a great similarity in the time usage of similar tasks, more weight should be given to the closest analogy or analogies. When, on the other hand, there is a large variance in the time usage or productivity of similar tasks, more weight should be given to the average of a larger set of analogies.[3]

The following real-world case exemplifies what may happen if the closest analogies are not recognized as being unusual. A large governmental organization successfully completed a software development project. Everything went as planned, the project involved exceptionally skilled members, and productivity was well above typical levels for such projects. When a new, reasonably similar development project was planned, the organization used the time spent by this previously completed project as the time prediction of the new project. What happened? The new project was now more like a *normal* project, and the project suffered great cost and time overruns. The scope of the project even had to be reduced to avoid a huge failure. The use of closest analogies is a useful method, but be aware of its limitations.

Take home message 1: Explicit use of relevant past experience (analogies) may lead to accurate time predictions, especially when it is possible to identify analogies *very* similar to the task to be predicted. When no very similar analogies can be identified, decomposition-based time predictions may lead to more accurate time predictions.

Take home message 2: If uncertainty is high or the analogies identified are unusual, for example, with respect to productivity, the predictions should be adjusted towards the average time usage or productivity of a larger set of similar tasks.

7.3 Relative Predictions

It may sometimes be useful to predict how much more or less time a task will take *relative* to another task rather than predicting the task's time usage. When predicting the time needed to paint a house, we may, for example, judge that it will require twice as much time to paint wall B compared to wall A. This type of time prediction method is called relative time prediction and is, amongst others, used in software development time prediction contexts [13]. A main motivation for the method is the

---

[3]This 50–50 rule of thumb assumes that the correlation between the time usage of the closest analogy and the time usage of mountain trips of similar length is about 0.5. If, for example, the correlation was as high as 0.8, it might be better to predict the time usage as 0.8 times the analogy-based prediction plus 0.2 times the prediction based on a broader set of tasks. In the extreme case in which there is no correlation between the closest analogy and the new task, the predicted productivity should be based only on the average productivity of the broader set of tasks. The above rule of thumb includes a few assumptions, for instance about the variance of the variables, but may work well in many contexts.

belief that we are frequently better at predicting relative time usage than absolute time usage. Another motivation for relative time prediction is that it may be more robust with respect to *who* is doing the work. Assume that we do not yet know who will paint the walls and that people differ greatly in how fast they paint. Consequently, an absolute time prediction without knowing who the painter will be may be of little value, whereas a relative time prediction may still be useful, assuming that that the relative difference in time spent on the different walls is fairly constant across painters.

Relative predictions may be stated in *percentages*—for example, that painting wall A takes 200% (twice as much) of the time it takes to paint wall B—but may also be stated as *additive* relative predictions—for example, that wall B will take 30 work hours more than wall A. One challenge with the use of percentages was demonstrated in an experiment with software professionals. One group was asked to predict the time needed to complete project A as a percentage of the time required for project B and another group was to predict the time needed for project B as a percentage of the time required for project A. On average, the first group believed that project A was 78% of project B and the second group believed that project B was 70% of project A [14]. Clearly, it would be paradoxical if project A required less time usage than project B and, at the same time, project B required less time usage than project A. In the same study, another group of software professionals gave relative predictions in the form of differences in work hours. These predictions made more sense and suggested that people struggle more with getting the percentages than the differences right when predicting relative time. The disadvantage of using absolute differences (e.g. 30 hours more) instead of proportions (e.g. 30% more) is, however, that the time predictions become more person dependent.

A relative prediction process sometimes used by project planners is the *story points*-based time prediction method,[4] outlined below.

Time prediction based on story points

- Divide the work into manageable tasks, for example, tasks believed to take a maximum of one person-week.
- Pick one task, preferably one that is medium large and well understood by all experts, to be your *reference task* (or baseline task).
- Give the reference task a number of story points, for example, agree on 10 story points. The number of story points of the reference task is arbitrary and could be any number.
- Predict the time usage of all the other tasks relative to the reference task. If one task is believed to take half the amount of time it takes to complete the reference task (10 story points), it should be given five story points. A task that is believed to take 50% more time than the reference task should be given 15 story points and so on.

---

[4]The term *story points* is derived from the concept of user stories, which are short descriptions of what users want to achieve with the software to be constructed.

- Knowledge (or prediction) of the time usage of the reference task or knowledge about the typical productivity (story points per hour[5]) allows for the conversion of story points into actual time units, such as work hours, or how much a team is capable of completing the next week. Knowledge about the productivity may be derived from previous tasks, or based on feedback from actual productivity (e.g. story points per work day) of the first deliveries of the work.

There are few empirical studies on the benefits and drawbacks of *relative* time prediction methods compared to the more common *absolute* time prediction methods. Seemingly, there are contexts in which time prediction accuracy improves [15] and contexts in which it worsens when relative time predictions are given [16]. One general advice about relative time predictions is to be careful with and perhaps even avoid comparisons of tasks that differ substantially in size. The reason for this is that tasks are often perceived as more similar than they actually are (assimilation effect). A task that is, in reality, 10 times larger than the reference task may consequently be more underestimated when using relative instead of absolute time prediction methods.

Take home message 1: Relative time prediction methods may simplify the prediction process and reduce the importance of knowing who is going to complete the work.

Take home message 2: Generally, relative time predictions do not seem to be more accurate than absolute time predictions. When tasks differ substantially in size, relative prediction methods may lead to prediction biases, such as underestimating larger tasks and overestimating smaller tasks.

7.4 Time Prediction Models

Historical data may be used to build formal (mathematical) models predicting the future. While researchers seem to enjoy developing complex prediction models, publishing hundreds of them in academic journals, there is surprisingly little evidence in favour of complex prediction models compared to simpler ones. In 97 comparisons between simple and complex prediction models (from domains other than time prediction), the complex models had no advantage when judged by the level of prediction accuracy [17]. Instead, the complex models increased the prediction error by 27%, on average. A simple model is defined here as one that the user understands how to apply, how previous outcomes have been represented in the model, how the relations are integrated in the model, and, finally, the relation between the model and the predictions.

Evaluations of the accuracy of prediction models in the domain of time prediction seem to arrive at the same result. We find no indication that complex models yield more accurate time predictions than simple models with few variables [18]. On the

---

[5]This productivity measure is typically called the *velocity* by those using this method.

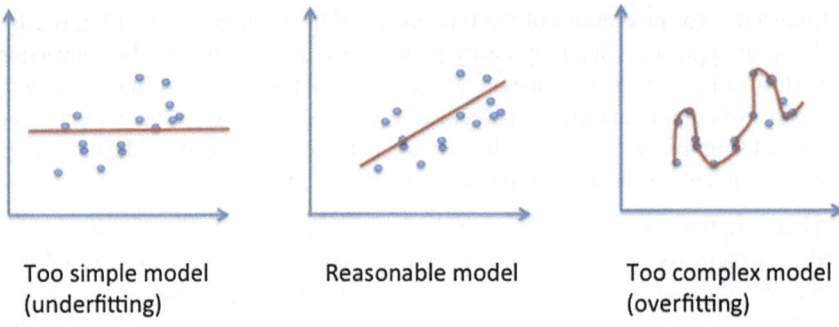

Too simple model   Reasonable model   Too complex model
(underfitting)   (overfitting)

Fig. 7.1 A model (red line) can fit the data points poorly (left), reasonably well (middle), and too well, leading to overfitting (right)

contrary, complex models tend to be less accurate in many realistic time prediction situations [19]. One likely reason for the lower accuracy of complex models is the lack of stable relations between important input variables, and the output (the predictions). For example, the effects of task size (e.g. number of requirements, features to be developed, steps to be taken) and task complexity (e.g. the number of workers to coordinate) on time usage seem to vary greatly across different work contexts. If such effects differs greatly across contexts and these differences are not properly modelled, the more complex time prediction models will tend to overfit the historical data. That is, the models become very good at explaining past time usage at the expense of their ability to predict the future. Illustrations of a too simple model, a reasonable model, and an overfitted model of the relation between task size (x-axis) and time usage (y-axis) are displayed in Fig. 7.1. If you ever encounter a time prediction model that uses terms you do not understand, such as *neural networks* or *fuzzy logic*, or that asks you to provide all kinds of detailed information about the task, it is usually a good idea to be sceptical; model overfitting is highly likely.

When developing a formal model to predict time usage, it is usually safest to use *local* data, such as data from your own context, the organization where you work, or at least data from very similar contexts [20]. Time prediction models intended to be applicable across a range of contexts are typically less accurate [19].

The following is an example of how the ingredients of a simple local time prediction model can be derived:

1. Identify a meaningful measure of the *size* of the work, for example, pages to be written, tests to be graded, or features to be developed for your particular context.
2. Identify a meaningful categorization of the *complexity* of the work. This should correspond to identifying contexts with significantly different levels of productivity, for example, pages with simple versus complex content, multiple choice tests versus essays to be graded, and software features involving presentation only versus interactive features.

3. Obtain the actual time usages, preferably from local historical data, for the above-
mentioned components.

Based on the above ingredients, we may, for example, develop the following very
simple test-grading time prediction model.

- Our size measure is the number of tests.
- A meaningful categorization of the complexity of the test grading is multiple
choice (M) and essay (E).
- Historical, local (in this case, from the person conducting the test) data suggest that
we need, on average, five minutes to grade a multiple-choice test and 15 minutes
for an essay. In addition, we typically need 10 minutes for general preparation.
- The final model is then as follows: time usage (in minutes) $= 10 + 5 \times M + 15 \times E$.
- A prediction of how long it will take to grade five multiple choice tests and seven
essays is then $10 + 5 \times 5 + 15 \times 7 = 140$ minutes.

As pointed out earlier, adding more complexity to time prediction models does
not often pay off. You should consequently have good reasons to add many more
variables or implement more complex relations to your time usage prediction model.

What if the work to be predicted is so special that you have no relevant historical
data? Or what if you did not bother to collect any data before now? A good solution,
when feasible, is to *start the work* to see how productive you are and then try to
extrapolate from the data collected in the first stage of your work. This technique
is advocated by software professionals in the NoEstimates movement [21]. This
movement argues that most time predictions are a waste of time and even harmful.
It argues that, instead of making time predictions, one should measure progress and
extrapolate this progress to determine when tasks will be finished.[6] In spite of the
unrealistic suggestion that people should stop requesting and giving time predictions
before a project starts, it is indeed a good idea to extrapolate time usage from the first
stage to predict the time usage of the remaining work. Essentially, the NoEstimates
movement advocates the use of a simple time prediction model based on highly local
data. Few, if any, time prediction models are better than that.

Sometimes we know in advance that time prediction models will perform poorly.
This includes situations with so-called *broken leg information*.[7] Broken leg information is very specific information about a task that makes the average of previous
performance less diagnostic of future performance. Knowledge that a person's leg is
broken should, for example, lead to a radical change in predictions of how quickly
that person will walk to work from home. Similarly, if we know that a worker is
extremely skilled and experienced, our model based on the average productivity of
the typical worker will not work well.

It is sometimes difficult to know whether one is facing a broken leg situation, and
it is important to avoid thinking that most situations are special. Human judgement

---

[6]This is actually a type of time prediction.

[7]The introduction of broken leg information (broken leg cues) and a discussion on the need to
sometimes deviate from history-based predictions is described in Paul Meehl's famous paper from
1957 [22].

about *when* a model is valid is essential in many time prediction contexts. 'Know when to hold' em and know when to fold 'em', to quote words of wisdom from Kenny Roger's song "The Gambler".

Take home message 1: Unless there is strong evidence in favour of complex formal time prediction models, use a simple model.

Take home message 2: Collect data from your own context (local data) to build the models. If no such data are available, use data from very similar contexts.

Take home message 3: Judge whether any information about the task makes the use of the model invalid. On the other hand, do not think that most cases are special and thus qualify as broken leg situations.

7.5 Consider Alternative Futures

One method that has been suggested for increasing the realism of time predictions is to think about what can go wrong and try to recall difficulties in past tasks. This approach has an intuitive appeal, because a typical explanation for cost and time overruns is people's failure to take problems and difficulties into account. Still, at least two studies attempting to exploit the strategy of recalling a problematic past or imagining a problematic future have been unable to document improvements in time predictions [23, 24].

A few studies have even suggested that the opposite may happen. People urged to identify more reasons for failures or more risks factors may produce even more optimistic time predictions than those identifying fewer such reasons,[8] see also [26]. This result is not as strange as it sounds and similar results have been found for a range of other types of judgements. If it is easy to come up with negative information, such as when asked for only one reason for failure or the three most important risk factors, then one might think that this is a particularly problematic project, since it is so easy to come up with the reason or risk factors. When, on the other hand, it is hard to come up with reasons for failure, such as when asked to come up with 12 or as many as possible reasons for failure, one may use the difficulty in finding the *last* reasons as an indication of the overall risk. If you feel that it is very hard to come up with the last reasons for failure, you may use this perception as an indication that failure is unlikely and thus make more optimistic time predictions. Thus, identifications of a large number of risk factors may affect time predictions in unexpected ways.

Let us try a small experiment. Predict the number of minutes you need to read the next 10 pages of this book. Do not read on before you have made a prediction.

Now, make a *new* time prediction about the same reading task, but assume that nothing unexpected will happen, that there will be no interruptions, and that there will be no need to reread parts that are difficult to understand.

---

[8]See [25]. Note that several later papers by the first author were retracted due to fraud.

Table 7.1 Example of a sequence of time predictions for one individual

Day	Time prediction	Actual time usage
1	15 minutes	19 minutes
2	17 minutes	Failed/gave up
3	16 minutes	27 minutes
4	16 minutes	18 minutes
5	17 minutes	26 minutes
6	18 minutes	15 minutes
7	13 minutes	14 minutes

Did you arrive at a different time prediction for the second, best-case situation? If you are like 25% of the participants in a similar experiment [27], you did not update the time prediction at all and, if you are like most of the other participants, it is likely that the difference between your first and second predictions is very small and not likely to reflect the real difference between a realistic and a best-case situation. What we think is a realistic outcome tends to be too close to the best-case outcome. This finding is not restricted to time predictions and is present in many types of predictions, for example, predicting how often one will exercise in the coming weeks [28].

In an unpublished study, we asked students to predict the time required to solve Sudoku (a type of number placement puzzle) tasks. All the Sudoku tasks were of similar complexity, the participants had experience in solving them, and we did not expect much learning or improvement from one Sudoku task to another. The students first predicted the time usage for a Sudoku task, then completed the Sudoku task, and finally received feedback about the actual time usage. This was done for several Sudoku tasks over seven days. An interesting time prediction pattern emerged that can be phrased as follows: *The future me is as good or better than the historically best me*—not the average, not the worst, but the best me. An example of a typical student's time predictions and actual time usage is given in Table 7.1.

The initial time prediction of the student was not really bad, just a bit low. The second time prediction assumed a performance better than the first day, perhaps based on the assumption of learning. In reality, the student failed completely at the task (the maximum available time was 60 minutes). In spite of this, the student believed that the next performance would be even better than that predicted the day before. The following days, until day six, the student systematically used more time than predicted but still believed that his performance would be a better than what he did at his best. On day six, the student spent less time on the task than predicted and immediately updated the time prediction to something even better than his new best performance. This student was not alone in thinking that his best performance was the most likely outcome for the next task. Many of the other students had this tendency in their time predictions, as well. This tendency towards insufficient differentiation of the ideal, best-case situation, where everything goes as planned, and the most likely case, where a normal amount of disturbances and problems occur, is likely to contribute to the amount of overoptimistic time predictions [23, 27].

One successful approach for dealing with this tendency seems to be to force a more explicit contrasting of the ideal and most likely outcomes. In short, one first asks for a time prediction given an ideal (best-case) situation and describes what an ideal situation means (lack of disturbance, no unexpected problems and optimal productivity), then one asks for the most likely (or realistic) use of time. This setup seems to make people understand that their time prediction of the most likely outcome should differ from the best-case scenario and they will therefore make higher and often more realistic time usage predictions.

In a study with software development professionals, this technique increased the time predictions by 30%, which, in that particular context, led to more realistic predictions [27]. Higher time predictions do not always mean more accurate predictions, but if you have a friend who is typically late or a team that typically underestimates time usage, try asking for the ideal-case prediction first and then require a most likely time usage prediction.

Take home message 1: Imagining alternative negative scenarios, such as possible reasons for failure and risk factors, does not seem to improve the accuracy of time predictions.[9]

Take home message 2: People have a tendency to give predictions of most likely time usages that are the same or too close to those given when instructed to assume best-case or ideal conditions. In short, what we think is realistic time usage tends to be too close to the best-case time usage.

Take home message 3: Imagining and predicting time usage assuming ideal conditions before predicting most likely time usage tends to lead to higher and, in many contexts, more accurate time predictions.

7.6   Combinations of Time Predictions

We once asked our students to predict the height of the Royal Palace in Oslo, Norway. Before looking at the students' predictions and not knowing the actual height of the Royal Palace, we made the following bet with them: Our prediction, which will be the median value of your predictions, will be as good as or closer to the actual value than at least half of your predictions. Why is this bet very safe?

Twelve students participated in the bet and gave the following predictions (in increasing order): 10, 15, 15, 20, 21, 23, 30, 40, 60, 75, 120, and 370 metres. The median of these numbers is 26.5 metres. This turns out to be very close to the actual height of the Royal Palace, which is 25 metres. Our prediction was consequently not only more accurate than most of the students' predictions, but more accurate than *all* of them. Admittedly, the median of a group of predictions is seldom better than all

---

[9]This point should, of course, not be used to argue against systematic risk analyses and assessments of how risk factors affect the uncertainty of projects, which are very useful for project planning and management.

the predictions, as in this case, but our bet that the median would beat at least half of the predictions was very safe. In fact, the median prediction will *always* be as good as or better than half of the predictions used to calculate the median.

This mathematical fact may be demonstrated as follows:[10] The worst case for the median (our prediction) is that the actual value is more than or less than all the predictions made by the students. In that case, the median will be better than exactly 50% of the predictions. If, for example, the actual height of the Royal Palace is only nine metres, the median will be better than exactly 50% (30, 40, 60, 75, 120, and 370 metres) of the 12 individual predictions. In all the other cases, where the actual height lies somewhere within the range of predictions, the median will be more accurate than at least 50% of the individual predictions. If, for example, the actual height were 125 metres, the median of 26.5 metres would be better than seven of the predictions (10, 15, 15, 20, 21, 23, and 370 metres).

Research studies in construction planning, economic forecasts, patient survival rates, and many other areas all demonstrate that prediction accuracy tends to increase with the use of combined predictions.[11] This research also suggests that combinations using the median or the *trimmed mean* (mean when, e.g., the 25% highest and 25% lowest predictions are removed) are typically more accurate than using the mean of the predictions [30]. In the example where the students predicted the height of the Royal Castle, we see that the mean of the students' predictions would be less accurate due to the influence of a couple of very high predictions, whereas a trimmed mean, for instance, removing the two lowest and two highest predictions, would be pretty accurate.

The benefits of combined time predictions depend on the individual predictions being fairly *independent* of each other. When predictions are influenced by the same misleading factor, the same shortcoming of the time prediction method, or the same narrow experience of those making the predictions, the advantage of combining the predictions will be greatly reduced. Furthermore, when we have good reasons for believing that some experts are systematically and substantially more accurate than others, we should rely on their predictions or at least weight their predictions more than those of the others; that is, we should not ignore that the 'wisdom of smaller, smarter crowds' may be better than the 'wisdom of crowds'.[12] When, however, it is difficult to know who is systematically and substantially more accurate, as in most

---

[10] Although the explanation is simple, the accuracy of the median prediction has surprised and fascinated many, starting perhaps with Sir Francis Galton. See Galton's 1907 discovery that the median (not the mean, as often claimed) prediction of the weight of an ox, including many non-experts' judgments, were better than the predictions of the experts (see [29]).

[11] See [30]. The review in this paper found an improvement in prediction accuracy for all 30 contexts studied. The average improvement in prediction accuracy was 12.5%.

[12] The idea of *vox populi* (the voice of the people) is that even the predictions of people with low expertise will lead to good predictions when their predictions are combined. This idea, originating with Galton, has been repeated in the best-selling book *The Wisdom of Crowds* by James Surowiecki [31]. Most of the research suggests, however, that smaller groups with more qualified people result in better predictions. Clearly, it would be strange if combining many unqualified predictions would guarantee a qualified prediction. See [32]. See also [33].

time prediction contexts, it is better to stick with the median or the trimmed mean of all the predictions.[13]

So far, we have only talked about *mechanical combinations* of time predictions, that is, calculated combinations of independent, individual time predictions. What about the role of *discussions* and *groups* in combining predictions? While most people seem to believe that groups usually improve the quality of judgements, for example, through meetings, psychologists have long held the view that groups tend to decrease the quality of judgements. Business managers, for example, like to solve problems in meetings and to generate new ideas through brainstorming sessions. Psychologists, on the other hand, report that brainstorming in groups is not a good idea [35]. Who is right?

There are good reasons to be sceptical about predictions based on group discussions. It is well documented that group discussions sometimes lead to the censorship of opinions and so-called *groupthink*, where the desire to get along with the group's members leads to a preference for arguments that have already been expressed in the group [36]. There are, however, also cases in which group discussions are reported to produce better judgements, such as when trying to detect lies [37]. How about group discussions in the realm of time predictions? Will time predictions by groups reflect the madness or the wisdom of crowds?[14]

A number of potential effects seem to be involved in determining the effect of group discussions on time predictions. A series of studies on undergraduate students confirms the pessimistic view that information sharing is biased [39]. Time predictions produced by groups of students were more overoptimistic than the typical predictions given by individuals, perhaps because the group discussions focused on factors related to successful completion and less on potential negative factors.

In contrast, studies on groups of software professionals predicting the time usage of a development project produced results in favour of group-based predictions. The software professionals predicted the time usage individually (before engaging in group discussions), then contributed to a consensus-based time prediction in small groups of experts, and finally made individual predictions (after the group discussion). Both the group-based time prediction and the individual time predictions made after the group discussions were higher and more realistic than the individual time predictions made before the group work [34]. Based on qualitative analyses of the discussions, it seemed as if the groups were able to identify a larger set of activities that needed to be taken into account. The mechanical combination of judgements improved the time prediction accuracy compared to the individual time predictions, but the group-based time predictions improved the accuracy even further in this particular context.

---

[13] See [34]. Note that, when there are few, perhaps only two or three time predictions to combine, the mean will be the only meaningful way to combine them.

[14] This refers to two famous books on judgments in groups. The first one was published in 1841 and suggested that groups are very poor decisions makers. See [38]. The other book was published in 2004 and suggested the opposite, that groups make surprisingly good judgments and decisions. See [31].

Planning poker is an example of a structured method for time prediction in groups, inspired by the Delphi method [13, 40]. The following steps are typical steps in a time prediction game of planning poker:

1. The participants write down their individual (independent) time predictions on a card or choose premade cards with the appropriate numbers.
2. The participants simultaneously show their cards to each other (thus, the participants are not affected by each other and their initial predictions remain independent).
3. The participants, in particular those with the highest and lowest time predictions, justify and explain their time predictions.
4. The participants discuss their differences and new insights.
5. Steps 1–4 are repeated until a consensus or a fixed number of iterations (e.g. three) has been reached. If no consensus is reached, a mechanical combination using the median, trimmed mean, or mean of the predictions is used.

A study of the use of the planning poker method in a real-world software development context found that it decreased the median time prediction error (measured as the deviation from the actual use of time) from 50 to 33% [41]. An additional benefit was that the structured group-based time prediction led to a better and shared understanding of the work and its risks.

The use of combined predictions is also relevant to uncertainty assessments, as in deriving realistic prediction intervals. In a study of different strategies for combinations of uncertainty assessments in a software development context, group discussions generated prediction intervals that were more accurate than mechanical combinations of the intervals [42].

Take home message 1: The median of several time predictions is always more accurate than at least half—and usually more—of the individual time predictions.

Take home message 2: Unless you have good reasons to believe that the source of one of the time predictions is systematically and substantially more accurate than the other sources, use the median or the trimmed mean of several time predictions.

Take home message 3: Combinations of independently produced time predictions usually give better predictions than combinations affected by each other or that have common influences.

Take home message 4: Structured group discussions are likely to improve the time prediction accuracy, especially when discussions lead to the identification of more activities and potential challenges.

7.7 Let Other People Make the Prediction?

Results from research in social psychology suggest that other people, typically referred to as *observers*, tend to provide less biased time predictions than those who will actually complete the task, typically referred to as *actors*. The underlying idea is that actors are personally involved, motivated to finish quickly, and consequently biased. In contrast, observers have no stake in the performance and will tend to give more objective and less overoptimistic time predictions.

The results from a study on students and their assignments support this argument. The study found that those who were required to hand in the assignment (the observers) tended to be overoptimistic, but those who predicted the completion date for another student (the actors) were not [9]. The *actors* believed they would complete the work an average of 1.3 days earlier than they did. The *observers*, who predicted the completion time of other students, were too pessimistic and predicted a delivery time an average of 1.7 days later than the actual delivery time. Thus, observers may be less optimistic, but not necessarily more accurate.

When it comes to the prediction of time usage—and not completion times, as in the study above—the improvement by use of observers instead of actors is even less clear. One study found no difference in accuracy or bias between predictions of how long the actors themselves would spend building a computer stand and predictions of how long the average person would take [23]. Another study, predicting time usage in voicemail operations, found that observers with a high level of experience were even more optimistic than novices performing the task, whereas intermediate observers, perhaps with a better recollection of the difficulties of learning the operations, were more realistic [24].

There are often good reasons for letting people predict the time usage of their own work. In particular, this is the case when people know a great deal about *how* they plan to solve a task and *how much* time they have spent on similar tasks in the past. Several studies on software development have shown, perhaps for this reason, that predicting one's own time usage is associated with higher accuracy and with no increase in the level of optimism compared to predictions of other people's work [43, 44].

Judgements by observers may be more accurate than those by actors when assessing the *uncertainty* of time predictions, such as predictions of confidence intervals of time usage. This seems to be the case particularly when historical information on past prediction accuracy is available. One study found software developers to be strongly overconfident about the accuracy of their time predictions for their own tasks even with historical prediction accuracy information easily available, whereas observers, in this case other software developers, gave much more realistic uncertainty assessments based on the same information [45]. It seems as if actors tend to emphasize their specific knowledge about how to solve the task and neglect information about their previous time prediction accuracy. Observers, on the other hand, have little to rely on besides past time prediction accuracy. Information about previous time prediction accuracy is, as argued earlier, typically a better indicator of time prediction uncertainty than knowledge about how the specific task will be carried out.

Take home message 1: Actors, that is, those completing the tasks, tend to give more optimistic time predictions than observers in some contexts. Nevertheless, there are several contexts in where time predictions become more accurate when people predict the time usage of their own work rather than when the work is predicted by less involved observers. Generally, it may be better to let people predict the time usage of own work, especially when they have more knowledge about how to complete it and their previous productivity on similar tasks.

Take home message 2: Observers' time prediction uncertainty assessments seem to be more realistic than those of actors, especially when historical data about previous time prediction accuracy are available.

7.8   Removing Irrelevant and Misleading Information

At a seminar with software professionals, we once explained how arbitrary numbers (anchors) and other irrelevant information often influence our judgement. Following this introduction, the participants were asked to estimate the programming productivity of their last project. Before estimating their productivity, they were asked a question that included either an unreasonably high anchor ('Do you believe your programming productivity was less than 200 lines of code per hour on your last project?') or an unreasonably low anchor ('Do you believe your programming productivity was more than one line of code per hour on your last project?'). They were also warned that this question was meant to mislead them and that they should try to be as realistic as possible. Do you think the information they received about the anchoring effect along with the explicit warning removed the anchoring influence?

The information did not even come close to removing the effect of the anchors. Those with the low anchor thought that their productivity on the last project had been, on average, 12.4 lines of code per hour, while those in the high-anchor group thought that their productivity had been about three times higher, 35.2 lines of code per hour. Actually, the warnings did reduce the anchoring effect somewhat. A third group of participants, without the initial teaching and warnings, were even more affected by the same anchor manipulations.[15]

This anchoring result is similar to numerous other disappointing results on how difficult—perhaps impossible—it is to remove biases stemming from misleading and irrelevant information [47]. Not only is it difficult to reduce the effect of misleading information through instructions to ignore it, even more elaborate means to reduce bias do not seem to be of much help either. In a study on software professionals, we found that methods such as highlighting the relevant text and removing/hiding the irrelevant information by crossing it out with black ink did not remove all of the biasing effect on the time predictions.[16] The only safe way to avoid being affected by misleading or irrelevant information is, consequently, to completely avoid it, for example, by letting another person filter out misleading and irrelevant information before the time predictions are made. Thus, a useful time prediction technique or

---

[15]The results are described in [46].

[16]See [48]. The crossing out the irrelevant information method did, however, work much better than the highlight the relevant information method.

principle is simply to remove irrelevant information and neutralize misleading information before those in charge of the time prediction receive it.

Take home message: No known method can be used to remove the influence of irrelevant and misleading time prediction information, such as prediction anchors. The only method that works is to avoid exposure to such information. This may, for example, be accomplished by having another person remove irrelevant information and neutralize misleading information.

7.9   From Fibonacci to T-Shirt Sizes: Time Predictions Using Alternative Scales

In many contexts, we only need a rough prediction of how much time an activity will take. To avoid spending time on deriving time predictions with higher precision than needed, it may be useful to make predictions at less precise scales or use approximate task size categories. The following are examples of scales and categories sometimes used for this purpose:

- The Fibonacci-inspired scale (where the two previous values are added to determine the next value), with increasing differences between the numbers: 1, 2, 3, 5, 8, 13, 21, ...
- The base 2 scale with even more increasing differences between the numbers: 1, 2, 4, 8, 16, 32, 64, ...
- The 10 × scale: 10, 20, 30, 40, 50, ...
- The T-shirt categories: X-small, small, medium, large, and X-large, where each category is represented by a time value, for example, medium tasks take, on average, 20 h and large tasks, on average, 60 h.

When predicting time using an alternative scale, it is important to be aware of the *central tendency of judgement* [49] and of unintended loss of information. The central tendency of judgement tells us that we tend to be affected by what is perceived to be the middle of the chosen scale. The less we know about something and the greater the uncertainty, the more we are affected by the perceived middle value of the scale or interval we use. In many ways, this is a rational reaction to uncertainty (see the discussion on the magnitude bias in Sect. 5.5), but it may also lead to biased time predictions.

The scale effect was demonstrated in an experiment where we asked one group of students to use the linear (1, 2, 3, 4, ...) scale with numbers up to 40, which has the middle number 20. Another group of students used the Fibonacci-inspired, nonlinear scale 1, 2, 3, 5, 8, 13, 20, 30, 40, which has the middle number 8 [50]. The students were asked to predict the number of work hours they would use for a software development task using numbers from the scale they had been assigned. The students who used the linear scale gave a median time prediction of 20 hours, while those with the nonlinear scale gave a median prediction of only eight hours, which, in this context, was clearly too low. Mainly the least experienced participants were affected by the use of the nonlinear scale. The results consequently suggest that we should be careful when using nonlinear scales, especially in a context with high uncertainty and low experience. If, as in our study, the middle value of the alternative scale is lower than that of the linear scale, the choice of that scale will lead to lower time predictions, especially when the uncertainty is high.

When using time usage categories, such as in t-shirt estimation (e.g. small = 10 hours, medium = 40 hours, and so on), the effect of the middle category (the medium size) may be similarly strong. People tend to select the middle category when they do not really know what to predict or they think the uncertainty is high; that is, people sometimes use the medium or middle category as a replacement for 'I don't know'. Clearly, there is much power in deciding what is perceived as the middle value or category of a scale used for responses.

A scale's low *precision* may also lead to an unintended loss of information. Say, for example, that one knows, based on previous experience, a task takes 40 hours. Being forced to select between 32 and 64 hours in a base 2 scale or between a medium (20-hour) and a large (60-hour) task in t-shirt estimation may be unfortunate in this case. Consequently, if one has chosen to rely on such scales, it should be possible to deviate from the scale numbers when there are good reasons for it.

Nonlinear scales have been claimed to be more natural or intuitive than linear scales.[17] Even if this were true, the limited empirical evidence on this topic in time prediction contexts does not suggest that nonlinear scales lead to more accurate time predictions [50]. We have conducted several (unpublished) experiments on this topic, all with the same disappointing result that the use of nonlinear scales provides no clear accuracy benefits.

Take home message 1: The use of low-precision scales, such as Fibonacci-like scales, may speed up time prediction work.

Take home message 2: Do not expect the use of alternative scales, such as nonlinear scales, to improve time prediction accuracy.

References

1. Armstrong JS, Green KC, Graefe A (2015) Golden rule of forecasting: be conservative. J Bus Res 68(8):1717–1731
2. Jørgensen M (2004) Top-down and bottom-up expert estimation of software development effort. Inf Softw Technol 46(1):3–16

---

[17]Studies of indigenous cultures and small children suggest that our intuitive number system (approximate number system) is nonlinear, with increasing intervals at increasing magnitudes. This number system has several advantages. It is able to compress high numbers on a short numerical scale and it reflects the fact that a difference in one unit is more important for small numbers (2 vs. 3) than for large numbers (1000 vs. 1001). See, for example, [51].

3. Furulund KM, Moløkken-Østvold K (2007) Increasing software effort estimation accuracy using experience data, estimation models and checklists. In: IEEE seventh international conference on quality software, 2007. pp 342–347
4. Hadjichristidis C, Summers B, Thomas K (2014) Unpacking estimates of task duration: the role of typicality and temporality. J Exp Soc Psychol 51:45–50
5. Kruger J, Evans M (2004) If you don't want to be late, enumerate: unpacking reduces the planning fallacy. J Exp Soc Psychol 40(5):586–598
6. Buehler R, Griffin D (2003) Planning, personality, and prediction: the role of future focus in optimistic time predictions. Organ Behav Hum Decis Process 92(1):80–90
7. Forsyth DK, Burt CD (2008) Allocating time to future tasks: the effect of task segmentation on planning fallacy bias. Memory & Cognition 36(4):791–798
8. Connolly T, Dean D (1997) Decomposed versus holistic estimates of effort required for software writing tasks. Manage Sci 43(7):1029–1045
9. Buehler R, Griffin D, Ross M (1994) Exploring the 'planning fallacy': why people underestimate their task completion times. J Pers Soc Psychol 67(3):366–381
10. Tversky A (1977) Features of similarity. Psychol Rev 84(4):327–352
11. Clemen RT (1989) Combining forecasts: a review and annotated bibliography. Int J Forecast 5(4):559–583
12. Jørgensen M, Indahl U, Sjøberg D (2003) Software effort estimation by analogy and 'regression toward the mean'. J Syst Softw 68(3):253–262
13. Cohn M (2005) Agile estimating and planning. Pearson Education, NJ, USA
14. Jørgensen M (2013) Relative estimation of software development effort: it matters with what and how you compare. IEEE Softw 30(2):74–79
15. Fredriksen I (2009) Empirical research on relative and absolute effort estimation in software development projects. Master's thesis, University of Oslo
16. Haugen NC (2006) An empirical study of using planning poker for user story estimation. In: Proceedings of the conference on AGILE 2006 IEEE, Washington, DC, pp 23–34
17. Green KC, Armstrong JS (2015) Simple versus complex forecasting: the evidence. J Bus Res 68(8):1678–1685
18. Jørgensen M (1995) Experience with the accuracy of software maintenance task effort prediction models. IEEE Trans Software Eng 21(8):674–681
19. Jørgensen M (2007) Forecasting of software development work effort: evidence on expert judgement and formal models. Int J Forecast 23(3):449–462
20. Kitchenham BA, Mendes E, Travassos GH (2007) Cross versus within-company cost estimation studies: a systematic review. IEEE Trans Softw Eng 33(5)
21. Duarte V (2015) No estimates: how to measure project progress without estimating. Oikosofy
22. Meehl P (1957) When shall we use our heads instead of the formula? J Couns Psychol 4(4):268
23. Byram SJ (1997) Cognitive and motivational factors influencing time prediction. J Exp Psychol Applied 3(3):216–239
24. Hinds PJ (1999) The curse of expertise: the effects of expertise and debiasing methods on prediction of novice performance. J Exp Psychol Applied 5(2):205–221
25. Sanna LJ, Parks CD, Chang EC, Carter SE (2005) The hourglass is half full or half empty: temporal framing and the group planning fallacy. Group Dyn Theory Res Pract 9(3):173–188
26. Jørgensen M (2010) Identification of more risks can lead to increased overoptimism of and over-confidence in software development effort estimates. Inf Softw Technol 52(5):506–516
27. Jørgensen M (2011) Contrasting ideal and realistic conditions as a means to improve judgment-based software development effort estimation. Inf Softw Technol 53(12):1382–1390
28. Tanner RJ, Carlson KA (2008) Unrealistically optimistic consumers: a selective hypothesis testing account for optimism in predictions of future behavior. J Consum Res 35(5):810–822
29. Galton F (1907) Vox populi (The wisdom of crowds). Nature 75(7):450–451
30. Armstrong JS (2001) Combining forecasts. In: Principles of forecasting, vol 30. International Series in Operations Research & Management Science. Springer, Boston, MA, pp 417–439
31. Surowiecki J (2004) The wisdom of crowds. Doubleday, New York

32. Goldstein DG, McAfee RP, Siddharth S (2014) The wisdom of smaller, smarter crowds. In: Proceedings of the fifteenth ACM conference on economics and computation. ACM, pp 471–488
33. Budescu DV, Chen E (2014) Identifying expertise to extract the wisdom of crowds. Manage Sci 61(2):267–280
34. Moløkken-Østvold K, Jørgensen M (2004) Group processes in software effort estimation. Empirical Softw Eng 9(4):315–334
35. Diehl M, Stroebe W (1987) Productivity loss in brainstorming groups: toward the solution of a riddle. J Pers Soc Psychol 53(3):497
36. Baron RS (2005) So right it's wrong: groupthink and the ubiquitous nature of polarized group decision-making. In: Zanna MP (ed) Advances in experimental social psychology, vol 37. Academic Press. San Diego, CA, pp 219–253
37. Klein N, Epley N (2015) Group discussion improves lie detection. Proc Natl Acad Sci 112(24):7460–7465
38. Mackay C (1841) Memoirs of extraordinary popular delusions and the madness of crowds. Routledge, London
39. Buehler R, Messervey D, Griffin D (2005) Collaborative planning and prediction: does group discussion affect optimistic biases in time estimation? Organ Behav Hum Decis Process 97(1):47–63
40. Linstone HA, Turoff M (eds) (1975) The Delphi method: techniques and applications, vol 29. Addison-Wesley, Reading, MA
41. Moløkken-Østvold K, Haugen NC, Benestad HC (2008) Using planning poker for combining expert estimates in software projects. J Syst Softw 81(12):2106–2117
42. Jørgensen M, Moløkken K (2002) Combination of software development effort prediction intervals: why, when and how? In: Proceedings of the 14th international conference on software engineering and knowledge engineering. ACM, pp 425–428
43. Jørgensen M (2004) Regression models of software development effort estimation accuracy and bias. Empirical Softw Eng 9:297–314
44. Lederer AL, Prasad J (1995) Causes of inaccurate software development cost estimates. J Syst Softw 31:125–134
45. Jørgensen M, Gruschke TM (2009) The impact of lessons-learned sessions on effort estimation and uncertainty assessments. IEEE Trans Software Eng 35(3):368–383
46. Mair C, Shepperd M, Jørgensen M (2014) Debiasing through raising awareness reduces the anchoring bias. ualresearchonline.arts.ac.uk/7334/1/BPS_Poster_2014_Mair_Shepperd_A0.pdf. Accessed May 2017
47. Løhre E, Jørgensen M (2016) Numerical anchors and their strong effects on software development effort estimates. J Syst Softw 116:49–56
48. Jørgensen M, Grimstad S (2008) Avoiding irrelevant and misleading information when estimating development effort. IEEE Softw 25(3):78–83
49. Hollingworth HL (1910) The central tendency of judgment. J Philos Psychol Sci Methods 7(17):461–469
50. Tamrakar R, Jørgensen M (2012) Does the use of Fibonacci numbers in planning poker affect effort estimates? In: 16th international conference on evaluation & assessment in software engineering (EASE 2012). IET, pp 228–232
51. Dehaene S, Izard V, Spelke E, Pica P (2008) Log or linear? Distinct intuitions of the number scale in Western and Amazonian indigene cultures. Science 320(5880):1217–1220

Chapter 8
Time Predictions: Matching the Method to the Situation

There are many time prediction methods and principles. How should we choose between them? Time prediction methods have advantages and disadvantages that depend on the situation, but there is a scarcity of useful guidelines on how to select time prediction methods. We attempt to provide some guidance in Fig. 8.1, with more detailed explanations of the questions and the time prediction method selection advices in the subsequent paragraphs.

1. **Do you have access to historical information about one or more similar previously completed tasks?**

   If you have access to data on time usage for similar tasks, you may use analogy-based time prediction methods (also known as *reference class forecasting*): Compare the characteristics of the new task with previously completed similar tasks and use the time spent on similar tasks as the predicted time on the new task. Studies on the use of analogy-based time predictions suggest that this approach mainly leads to high accuracy when the task to be predicted and one or more of the previously completed tasks are *very* similar [1]. If no data on very similar tasks are available but data on fairly similar tasks exist, the median or trimmed mean value of a larger set of fairly similar analogies (or the mean when only few analogies are identified) usually provides a good prediction.

2. **Do you have information about previously completed tasks and evidence supporting a stable relation between task characteristics and time usage?**

   Information about past tasks may be used to create simple formal models of the relations between the task's characteristics and time usage. Such models may work well when there are good measures of the task's key characteristics (such as its size and complexity), when these characteristics are known before the task starts, and when we have data about key performance variables, such as the productivity of those who will complete the task. In addition, it is essential that the relations included in the model, such as that between task size and time spent, be reasonably stable. This does not mean that variations in productivity over time have to be problematic. For instance, when the average time to replace a window (say, 40 minutes) is stable, it

© The Author(s) 2018
T. Halkjelsvik and M. Jørgensen, *Time Predictions*, Simula SpringerBriefs on Computing 5, https://doi.org/10.1007/978-3-319-74953-2_8

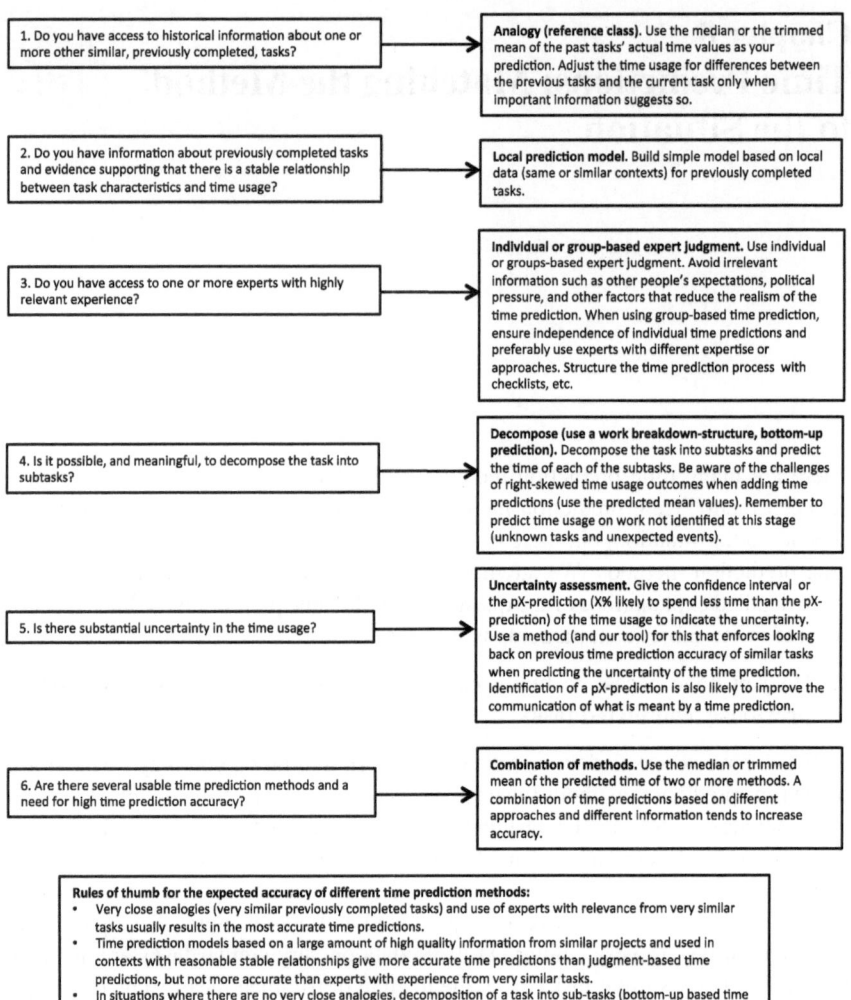

Fig. 8.1 A guide to selecting time prediction methods

does not matter whether it sometimes takes 20 minutes and at other times 90 minutes if the job is to replace 500 windows. Across many occasions, noise (e.g. bad or good luck) cancels itself out and your future average time usage will probably be close to your past average time usage, given a similar type of work and similarly skilled workers.

We are not aware of any general formal—often termed parametric—model that is valid across many time prediction contexts. The likely reason for this is the lack of highly predictive variables and stable time usage–related relations across different situations. It is possible but unlikely that we will come across examples of successful general formal time prediction models in the future and you should currently be highly suspicious if someone claims that their time production model is useful across a large number of situations. Models derived from past time usage data in your *local* context work better. Simple models are also often more accurate than complex models, probably due to less overfitting to the historical data.

3. Do you have access to one or more experts with relevant experience?

Expert judgements by people with *relevant* experience seem, on average, to be at least as accurate as predictions derived from formal time prediction models [2]. Be aware that the length of experience is a poor indicator of time prediction accuracy and that it is the *relevance* of the experience that matters most. This relevance quickly decreases with lack of similarity between past work and the task to be predicted.

When using expert judgement–based time predictions, it can be useful to accomplish the following:

(a) Remove irrelevant and misleading information, including information that may lead to social/organizational/political pressure, *before* sending the task information to those responsible for predicting time. Attempts to debias people exposed to irrelevant or misleading information, for example, by presenting more realistic time prediction anchors to counter the misleading one, may help but are usually not sufficient to remove the effect of the misleading information [3].

(b) Provide support and structure by using documented time prediction processes (e.g. planning poker), checklists [4], and templates for work breakdown structure.[1]

(c) Require time predictions to be justified by references to previous time usage.

4. Is it possible and meaningful to decompose tasks into subtasks?

Time predictions based on decomposition may give the most accurate time predictions and be the only viable option in contexts where very similar analogies cannot be found [1]. To enable accurate decomposed time predictions, there are several issues to be aware of, as follows:

- It is easy to forget to predict time spent on subtasks or activities that you are unaware of when you predict time, that is, on *unknown subtasks and unexpected events*. The best prediction of this is the proportion of time spent on such activities in the past.
- The right-skewed nature of time usage means that *adding* the time predictions of subtasks to find the total time usage should *not* be based on predictions of the *most likely* time usage but, instead, on the predicted *mean* time usage for each subtask. This requires information about the uncertainty of time usage.
- Some subtasks may be better predicted as a proportion of other subtasks rather than directly. For example, the time required for administration may be predicted as a proportion of the non-administrative tasks. Remember that the proportion of administration increases with increasing team and project size.

---

[1]For a general guide, see [5].

- Risk analysis, that is, the identification and assessment of events that may affect the time usage, should be an integral part of the time prediction process, not a separate activity. The risk analysis should be used as input to calculate the expected amount of extra time usage due to the risk factors.
- Dependencies between activities and between risks should be modelled. This includes modelling multiplicative dependencies between activities and correlations between risks. Monte Carlo simulations may be used for this purpose.[2]

5. **Is there substantial uncertainty in the prediction of time usage?**

Include an assessment of the uncertainty of the time usage, for instance, by the use of time prediction intervals. This will make it easier to communicate the range of possible time usage outcomes and is useful for planning and budgeting purposes. Uncertainty assessments may also be used to give predictions a more precise meaning through pX time predictions (e.g. p80 equals an 80% chance of not exceeding the prediction). It is essential to avoid uncertainty assessment methods that lead to strongly overconfident (too narrow) time prediction intervals, since they may do more harm than good.

6. **Are there several feasible time prediction methods and a need for high time prediction accuracy?**

The accuracy of time predictions may be improved by combining time predictions from different sources and using different prediction methods. *Mechanical* combinations using the median, the trimmed mean (excluding a proportion of the lowest and highest predictions), or the mean (when few time predictions are available and there are no outliers) of time predictions from different sources are possible methods for this. A proper *group-based* combination is typically based on a process in which experts individually predict the required time and then discuss and share these predictions and their rationale. Based on the discussion, the experts may choose to update their time predictions. In the final stage, the group agrees on a time prediction or uses a mechanical combination of the individual predictions. Especially for tasks where the discussion and sharing of knowledge are essential for accurate predictions, group-based combinations are likely to improve time prediction accuracy more than mechanical combinations are. The benefit of combining time predictions, regardless of the combination approach, strongly depends on the independence of the individual time predictions. If there are good reasons to weight one method more than the other, one may choose to do so; otherwise, it is better to weight all the time predictions equally.

---

[2]This can be done in the free software Riscue: http://www.riscue.org/.

References

1. Jørgensen M (2004) Top-down and bottom-up expert estimation of software development effort. Inf Softw Technol 46(1):3–16
2. Jørgensen M (2007) Forecasting of software development work effort: evidence on expert judgement and formal models. Int J Forecast 23(3):449–462
3. Løhre E, Jørgensen M (2016) Numerical anchors and their strong effects on software development effort estimates. J Syst Softw 116:49–56
4. Jørgensen M, Moløkken K (2003) A preliminary checklist for software cost management. In: Proceedings of IEEE third international conference on quality software, 2003. pp 134–140
5. NASA (2016) Work Breakdown Structure (WBS) Handbook. ntrs.nasa.gov/archive/nasa/casi.ntrs.nasa.gov/20160014629.pdf

Chapter 9
How to Obtain Overoptimistic Time Predictions from Others

Below is a list of elements describing how to get low time predictions, ranked by what we believe is their magnitude of impact. The elements are likely additive, where combinations of more elements may further lower the time predictions. However, the effect of adding biases has not been studied much, so we do not know how bad things can get in such combinations. The list is meant to be a *warning* about how the person requesting a time prediction can easily contribute to overoptimism. That person could be you, for example, in the role of the client or project manager or when asking a carpenter about the time needed to remove an interior wall in your home. If, in spite of our warning, you include one or more of the elements described here to manipulate other people's time predictions, you have only yourself to blame for low work quality, frustrated coworkers, increased coordination costs, and missed deadlines.

Optimism-inducing time prediction request elements:

1. Exploit the use of *prediction anchors*. Anchoring effects are extremely robust and the moment a person is exposed to an anchoring value, that person will have a hard time avoiding being affected. There are many ways to introduce low time prediction anchors. One way is to ask questions such as 'do you think it will take more than _____?' (a number representing a low use of time). Another way is to indicate an initial low budget or little time available, such as 'I have only _____ (a number representing a low use of time or a low cost). Do you think that will be enough?'
2. Exploit the *selection bias* (winner's curse) effect by inviting several people to predict the time required and selecting among those with the lowest time prediction or the lowest price in a bidding round. You find the strongest selection bias when the number of time predictions to select from is high, when there is a large difference between the lowest and highest time predictions, when the expected prediction accuracy is low, and when the actual time to complete the work does not vary much across different workers.
3. Exploit the *sequence effect*. An initial time prediction will typically influence, as a reference, the next time predictions through the so-called assimilation effect.

© The Author(s) 2018
T. Halkjelsvik and M. Jørgensen, *Time Predictions*, Simula SpringerBriefs on Computing 5, https://doi.org/10.1007/978-3-319-74953-2_9

Requesting the time prediction of a small task before that of a larger task will consequently lower the prediction time of the larger task. The sequence effect may also be present if you select people who recently (or mainly, in the past) predicted time usages for smaller tasks.

4. Exploit the effects of *motivation*. The addition of incentives for a task's fast and efficient completion lowers time predictions more than the actual time usage. For instance, you could make it clear that a low time usage will lead to future opportunities or other benefits. You may also inform people that it is very important to complete the work within a short time period.

5. Exploit the effect of *updating time predictions*. A strategy to obtain lower time predictions is to first ask for the time prediction of a task with extra features (bells and whistles), that is, with many things you do not really need. Then ask for an update of the time prediction for a reduced version of the task, which will include only the features you actually need. The revised time prediction is likely to be too low.

6. Exploit the *framing and format effects*. How a time prediction is requested clearly matters and there are several ways to exploit request formats to lower a time prediction. One way is to frame the time prediction request using words associated with smaller or simpler tasks, for example, 'how much time do you need to complete this *simple* task?' Another way is to change the prediction request into a format such as 'how much can you complete in ____ hours?', where the number of hours is only a small proportion of the total time needed. A third alternative is to request the time prediction in a time unit that implicitly indicates that the task is small, for instance, request the time prediction in minutes when the task takes several hours or in hours when a task takes several months.